10887512

Walking on Fire

Walking on Fire

The Shaping Force of Emotion in Writing Drama

Jim Linnell

Southern Illinois University Press
Carbondale and Edwardsville

Printed in the United States of America

14 13 12 11 4 3 2 1

Library of Congress Cataloging-in-Publication Data
Linnell, James Ward.
Walking on fire : the shaping force of emotion in writing drama / Jim Linnell.
p. cm.
Includes bibliographical references and index.
ISBN-13: 978-0-8093-3047-8 (pbk. : alk. paper)
ISBN-10: 0-8093-3047-4 (pbk. : alk. paper)
ISBN-13: 978-0-8093-9066-3 (ebook)
ISBN-10: 0-8093-9066-3 (ebook)
1. Playwriting—Psychological aspects. 2. Language and emotions. 3. Drama—Technique. I. Title.
PN1661.L45 2011
808.2—dc22 2010052212

Printed on recycled paper. ♲
The paper used in this publication meets the minimum requirements of American National Standard for Information Sciences—Permanence of Paper for Printed Library Materials, ANSI Z39.48-1992. ♾

For Jennifer and the boys—Hadrian, Jason, and Matt

Contents

Acknowledgments

Patricia Mannion spent hours transcribing conversations between Digby Wolfe and me, conversations that were midwife to this book. Patricia's unfailing encouragement pushed the talk into real pages. I relied on the wisdom and experience of psychologist Dr. Samuel Roll, who, if he wasn't making me laugh or telling me useful stories from his experience, offered insights that helped ground the relationship between psychoanalytic theory and drama. My thanks to psychiatrist David Landau and psychologist Marcia Landau, his spouse, who introduced me to the work of the International Conference on Literature and Psychoanalysis. David and I jointly presented papers on two topics that became part of this book: Brecht's *Puntila and His Servant Matti* and Pinter's *Birthday Party.* Their generous and perceptive interest in this project was an unfailing source of support. My thanks to colleagues in the Department of Theatre and Dance at the University of New Mexico, who support the Writing Program, and to my students, who have contributed so much to my thinking about the process of writing and teaching. Thanks to my friend Jim Danneskiold, who took on the task of editing these pages with sympathy and conceptual clarity. Finally, my wife and friend, Jennifer, for her dim view of difficulty and her fearless belief in and embrace of the creative process and me. Our children are all in the arts, one in architecture and two in film. Our life together and their choices in making art give extra meaning to my journey as a writer engaged with this book. My son Matt particularly shares the task of walking on fire as a young screenwriter. All writing is personal, so, from father to son, may this work be a useful guide for him on the journey ahead.

Walking on Fire

Prologue

When I think of how this book began and was shaped, I start in a place. That place is the porch of my house beside the Rio Grande, south of Albuquerque. It is the late spring 1999. Two men, colleagues in the Dramatic Writing Program at the University of New Mexico, sit down to talk. Opposite me is Digby Wolfe. Digby came to New Mexico first as a visiting professor and then was hired as the chair of the Robert Hartung Dramatic Writing Program in the Theatre and Dance Department. During his time at UNM, he anchored the program with the depth and breadth of his professional experience and the quality of his teaching.

Not a year passed that the writing program, under his leadership and creative goading, didn't present a public festival or series of performances of original writing. Our offices sat across the hall from one another, and I can't think of Digby without hearing laughter and the sound of stifling convention shattering like glass. One day he brought writers on a team comedy project to his office to work out a scene. Soon the area around his office was ringing with laughter, of ideas howling at the moon, surprising, fearless, and unstoppable. It was the sound of Digby Wolfe at work.

When we began to circle the idea of a book, we agreed to meet to talk about our work with the writing students, our questions about how to teach writing, our connection over what we valued in writing, and how to elicit these values in our students especially through the examples we use in our classes. When we started, we didn't know if this was a one-day brainstorming or if it would find a way to continue. It was soon obvious that it was bigger. Before our first sip of coffee, we were deep in it, each throwing out ideas. Digby blazed with questions, with quotes from the library he carries in his head, and swift satirical jabs at the forces of stupidity, self-importance, and fear. I countered by channeling the Greeks, imagining Dionysus reanimating on the streets of Berkeley and, like a dog with a bone, holding onto the question, Why do we do what we do? That day we threw ideas on the table that we named Emotional Form or sometimes the Writer's Universe.

Digby emphasized his belief that emotional form must begin as the internal visceral process of the writer before it can grow into an organic structure in which the characters' emotions chart the architecture of the work. The best way to express this understanding, the best examples and descriptions grew out of where we diverged. We worked hard to join our approaches. Ultimately, we learned to respect the individuality of our visions. We decided to each seek our own separate path to that goal and the expression of the writer's process. I am grateful for Digby's friendship and his example of fierce contention and driving belief that marks everything he does. The heat generated in that contention has helped illumine and sharpen my own beliefs set out in this book.

You Are What You Write

Writing is not an abstraction. It is there in the life we've led, our experience. It is there in the "this is now" and "that is then" and in "who is or was closest to us." We are driven to write by our lived experience and our need to know what it means. For examples of emotional form, which is the conceptual framework of this work, I can point to books, to plays, to productions, to films, to comments on writing, but the crucial pointing is when we point at ourselves. A teacher can say, "Think about this," or "I lose the thread here," or "What if she does this," or "Clever, but it leaves me cold," or, simply, "Go deeper." You still have to go away and try one of these. The words and feelings will flow from you, a living person, not a technique or a literary device.

When we write, we tell our own stories over and over again. Not with the details of our biography but in the emotional experience, the choices made, the threats negotiated and persistent, the human knowledge that is the architecture of our lives. Self-study is everyone's practice when we shape stories. Whom do we know better? So the reader may ask, Who is writing this book? Why do I write plays, and why did I choose the theater as a career, become a teacher, and want to know why we do what we do?

The story I tell here as prologue is of a growing up, a story of beginnings that formed a direction, a purpose. My universe begins in New England, then creates its gravitational force around a professional life in the university. How did I form relationships between words and the world and words and myself, a journey to writing? Not from the head of Zeus but as offspring of a citizen farmer and a Victorian Eurydice, actually a country-lawyer father and a poet mother. The lawyer went public with all his words, and the poet kept all of hers to herself. Without knowing stage right from stage left, I became a player in a plot and played with the beginnings, middles, and ends of things. We lived in the country so I grew up as a little pagan whose catechism was the incantation of trees, water, animals, snow, and mud. Nature was like a mysterious marsh, a place where life was inextinguishable and death was everywhere and nowhere.

Two public stages were in my life: church, which was coolly Protestant, and the movie theater. In one public, the words of the King James Bible created a wind of language, stamped with ferocity and forgiveness. In the other public, this duality disappeared in the complexities of pleasure, pleasure of the flesh and of stories.

Usually, my grandmother, a tough Maine farmwoman who regretted leaving the gold fields of Colorado for a less-expansive New England, took me to the theater. She, too, anticipated the Westerns with some deep romance about the Rocky Mountains in her heart, a secret she kept from the Down East true believers.

The theater we sat in had a working stage and was part of a vaudeville circuit. So as we ate our popcorn before entering the heady world of horses, mountains, and, God help us, cowboys with guns, we saw the vaudeville show. One of the most popular acts was always the trained dogs—little poodles racing, leaping through hoops, standing on one leg, zipping between the bare legs of a woman in tight satin shorts who waved a silver wand. The crowd liked the tricks, the speed, the obedience to command, the eagerness to please, bared teeth and legs, a satisfying definition of love or art for the assembled small hosts. Then the film began, and we were plunged into the great open spaces, hard riding, hard justice, and soft women, with the after-image of white poodles, spinning tap dancers, and gleaming thighs.

The matinee excursions washed a montage over my wet brain of the mythic West, popular theater, my grandmother's yearning for a place, a geography that was meaningful, a lost past with possibly a terrible secret, the confusion of justice with the manipulation of helpless creatures. It is still there.

In my real life, the closest thing to theater was my father's world. He was a trial lawyer, a storyteller, a fisherman, and a family man, probably in that order. There was a kind of theater in progress at home. The play in which I was cast soon showed me conflict and action and the power of feeling over language: my father and brother wrestling on the back stairs over wayward teenage drinking; bared teeth and fists, yelling between the king and pretender, love and power. Then came the inevitable discovery of tragic word and subtext, lessons before dinner: a conversation suddenly hardening, mother in tears and dad possessing all the words, mother possessing the crushing power of silence.

Then there was the courtroom, as theatrical a place as the vaudeville with Grandma. The court seemed the embodiment of ceremony, dramatic machinery producing justice and misery in equal proportion. Imagine my surprise when I watched my father try a case to learn it was about sex, lying, risk, power, and plain stupidity. My father was representing the husband, who was suing his wife's lover for alienation of affections. I saw my father cross-examine the lover, caught like a bug in my father's questions. "And why exactly were you both sitting in the back seat of her car in her garage with her dress over your head?" This was comic opera, not crime and punishment.

We lived not far from the little town of Monmouth, where, as luck would have it, sat one of those jewel-like operetta theaters with ornate boxes on either side of the stage, everything curved and proportioned for a couple hundred patrons. One year, the American Savoyards of New York City decided to summer at this theater. It was my father's undoing. For the next three summers or so, we were regular patrons of their Gilbert and Sullivan repertoire. It was a revelation that adults laughed uncontrollably, appreciated all the pretty girls, singing, rhymed verse, costumes: all the seemingly useless pleasures.

I also associate my first contacts with theater with the day my father dropped me off at our local YMCA for my first swimming lesson. I was seven or eight years old. Probably twenty other boys arrived for the same purpose, descending with deafening anticipation down the stairs to the locker room next to the pool. Going to the Y for swimming was a big deal in my mind because swimming at the Y meant swimming naked. I don't know if this is still the practice, but I guess they were trying to teach the importance of the spirit over the flesh. This was a difficult line to cross at eight, never having been stark naked in a public place with a crowd of other boys my age. But there we were, a lot quieter than when our merry band careened down the stairs. We stood huddled together by the edge of the pool, arms across our scrawny chests, practicing the arts of serious pretense for the first time. We waited, performing airs of nonchalance and bravado, hiding our panic and embarrassment, acting as if it was normal to be naked in a room full of complete strangers getting ready to jump into freezing water. But jump we did and became both hidden and exhilarated.

What became significant was not my individual nakedness but my experience of a shared condition. All the efforts of the theater strive for this essential sight, to see our condition, however it may appear, no matter what language it speaks, however it moves from grace to horror to the luminously comic. Very little else about contemporary life teaches or allows this way of seeing.

Fishing created a connection to drama my father never intended. Fishing gave me a first glimpse into the world of men: who is in the circle and who is not, how language is used in trade for inclusion, and the threats to the whole, how politics is manifested. What I didn't know was that men did more than fish on these trips, and I would have to learn more than fishing to find my place among them.

At the camp were a dining lodge and simple cabins. At night at the lodge, the first order of business was a critique on the day's fishing and strategies for the next. The fly cases were opened and examined until it was settled what the trout, hidden from their will, wanted to eat. The men then drifted in a slow, unintended waltz, forming and reforming into knots of story telling, serious side conversations, and card playing. In the time before I entered the mists of puberty, the sound of this talk washed over me like a deep chant, taut with seductive force.

After I began dating and mirror gazing, their talk was no longer seductive but instead revealed the angular lines of personality coiled behind a scrim of chatter and cards. I now heard another strand, one of anger. It was just such an outburst that provided a connection with my father and taught me the incendiary mix of drama and character.

A doctor I'd known since I was old enough to play with his son blew into a rage about taxes, turning red as he railed bitterly against government. His hostility boiled loose from deep inside as he scorned the notion of giving up his money to the goddamned government. I expected my father to nod, even lead a chorus of agreement. He didn't. He was playing cribbage across the room and stood and walked over to the doctor. He was surprisingly angry. The room went quiet as the two men stood inches from each other. My father, after calling the doctor a damned jackass, made fun of the narrow selfishness of his tirade. He laughed at the doctor who wanted plenty from that stinking government, like roads, schools, security, and laws that allowed the doctor to make his heaping pile of cash. My father spoke, I realized, for people who weren't in the room. In this way, he addressed my muddled feelings about making my voice heard, about justice. I believe it was the only time outside of church or school that I heard an adult make an argument for the greater good, especially when it would actually cost him something.

Speaking one's mind was something willed; it was not simple or easy. I saw that to speak in the harsh glare of people's attention in opposition to another's will was transfixing. Exercising that will seemed like casting for the hidden trout, coaxing it to the surface by a language and purpose dressed to trick away fear and overcome selfish interests. My father helped me see how this trick floats above the ample waters of indifference. It was later that I saw that theater, at its core, seeks to perfect that same trick.

What happens when you don't have the language to reach the other? That lesson began a few years earlier. I'm standing in our driveway watching a stranger lead my mother's horse, a creature she held in her love as close, if not closer, than her children, out of the barn into a waiting trailer. She is also there, handkerchief gripped in her hand, as she watches in a kind of frozen panic. The man closes the trailer, and then I remember only silence except for the horse's hooves. The truck starts, the horse looks back at my mother, and the truck then glides out onto the road and away. She flees to her bedroom. For me, there is no erasing this image because it fits in a life-changing chain of events between my parents. This event came after an argument over whether to buy a summer cottage or sell the horses. My father made it an either or. My mother lost. Of course, it wasn't just about that choice. In fact, it grew from my father's affair, as his mistress was buying the camp next to ours. This event set in motion an unraveling, with its own emotional form, one that ended in a more desperate and cruel choice. I'm on the back deck of my flat in Berkeley in 1969 studying for my PhD exams. My brother calls to say our mother is dead. She took pills. We're saying it is a heart attack. Just come home. The math of loss just became more real, the equals sign more opaque and painful. An emotional form passed to me whose math is always with me.

Back in Berkeley, the daily political ritual in the streets kept getting uglier. I studied Bertolt Brecht and staged his earliest antiwar play, *Drums in the Night.* Weimar Germany of the 1920s and Berkeley of the 1960s became entangled in my mind. As students, we were immune from the draft for now. What scared us and what we wouldn't talk about was the world described by the character Kragler:

> What am I doing? Seasick on a sea that swarms with corpses but doesn't suck me down. Rolling southward in the dark cattle cars: nothing can happen to me. Burning in the fiery oven: I burn hotter myself. A man goes mad in the sun: not me. Two men fall into a water hole: I go on sleeping, I shoot blacks. I eat grass. I'm a ghost. (126)

I was in a rehearsal of this same play when the news broke that President Richard Nixon had invaded Cambodia, which felt like a direct attack on everyone protesting the war. It felt personal. People went nuts. My cast became unglued. Then the arguments started. We have to stop now, no business as usual. This is meaningless, like spitting into a furnace. Go to the streets, try to stop the system. I was furious at everything: at my own fear, at the lies, the posturing, at the effort to impose silence. I yelled, I threw a prop cane so hard it stuck in the wall; the play was going on, no matter what. So we did. It was a mess, but it didn't matter. I learned that theater isn't only about art. It comes from deep will and a need that is hidden in the visible event but fuels the creative process. My fury wasn't just about this play, I was furious about something beloved being taken away. I was doing my mother's math. Grappling thus with loss is never pretty. Emotion must come from this kind of work, not as a polite reminder of the how things could be, not as an ironic comment on life's quirks but in the hunt for the transforming power of emotion that needs no explanation, no excuse.

I passed my exams, I applied for teaching jobs. I received a call from a struggling new Black theater in a poor area for which I'd done some work. Was I free? Would I come back and work with the theater? That question, "Was I free?" still appears at night, like the ghost of Hamlet, haunting my purpose. At the same time, a university called and said, "Come, teach for us, and work in our theater." So I did.

The equation we create of child to family, to body, to nature, to words, to others, and to the never-equal pressure of external events is never done and always operates in the writer's mind and emotions. Every human and every writer wrestles with should I/shouldn't I, can I/can't I, will I/won't I—will and desire, success and failure, fear and courage. Never think you are free of this equation, especially if true writing is what you're after. The question is, How important is the world to you? *How* do you know that world? Does it foster in you a deep skepticism à la Brecht, a satiric elbowing à la Aristophanes or Nicky Sliver, or a feeling of awe at the deep mystery of human behavior à la Tony Kushner? Does your life have an emotional form? Emphatically, yes. And we are constantly trying to glimpse that form by telling our own stories: to lovers, to friends, to children, to ourselves.

My story can't be changed in fact, but it can be endlessly acted upon by my own discovery of its meaning. My writing is tied like Gulliver to my conflicts over loss, my desire to mend and to connect, my anger at what I don't understand and what I fear. Without that story and the way I newly understand it at each moment that I write, I'm neither the character that I am nor the writer that I am. Driven by the energy in the unresolved threats and conflicts of my past, I choose particular subject matter, I work toward endings that release my feelings about human relations. I strive in those endings to bring some small truth to the tension between cruelty and love. Your truth won't be the same, but it will address the tension between poles of feeling in your story. Dance around it if you must, but we all know that dance. That is why endings are hard. We go to the theater to see the dancer revealed.

Giving advice about writing can be a self-parodying process. Christopher Shinn presents an exchange between a writer, Dave, and his student in *What Didn't Happen.* The question asked by the student, Scott, is not just about his writing. Like an anxious palm reader, Dave gives an "get-me-out-of-this" answer often repeated in faculty-student encounters. The question not asked is the one that no one else can answer, Do I have the discipline?

SCOTT: But there's—one question I never asked you. Do you—and you can—do I have a future?

(*Pause.*)

DAVE: God. What a Question! Who can say. (*Beat.*) What's important is that you love to do it, and continue to do it, with discipline . . .

SCOTT: Uh-huh . . .

DAVE: You have to keep writing. And reading, all the time—and—then you'll find your own way. Your own path. But you're very young, Scott, so much will happen to you. Your life, your writing, will change in ways you can't fathom right now and—

SCOTT: —I know I'm not dumb, but—whatever it is that makes—like, I tell myself I should cut out TV and never read magazines and I think of all the books that I haven't read and it's like When Will I Read Them? Because I—like I *lack* something you *need* . . .

DAVE: I can relate! Everyone's full of doubts, trust me, we're all afraid we'll be found out for frauds—

SCOTT: —Aw, this is neurotic shit, isn't it?

DAVE: No—no. Of course you're going to wonder about the economic viability of writing as a career, it's practical thinking— (162)

Introduction

> Alice thought to herself, "I don't see how he can *ever* finish, if he doesn't begin." But she waited patiently.
>
> "Once," said the Mock Turtle at last, with a deep sigh, "I was a real Turtle."
>
> These words were followed by a very long silence, broken only by an occasional exclamation of "Hjekrrh!" from the Gryphon, and the constant heavy sobbing of the Mock Turtle. Alice was very nearly getting up and saying, "Thank you Sir, for your interesting story," but she could not help thinking there *must* be more to come, so she sat still and said nothing.
>
> —Lewis Carroll, *Alice's Adventures in Wonderland*

I come to this task, a professor and director/writer who has braved the crosswinds of the university and the classroom. The goals of my dramatic-writing students range from seeking an undergraduate education to a professional graduate degree or a playwriting career. I also come wind-burned by my own experiences of family, love, ambition, and conflicted self-knowledge. My experience in these settings energizes the convictions, arguments, and exhortations that emerge in this book.

There are stories about ourselves—as we were, or as we are, or as we would like to become—that create responses as real as our most intimate moments. Given the difficulties of writing and producing new plays, and the odds against earning a living as a playwright, it is worthwhile to give attention to those things that create the vital connections among writer, reader, performer, and audience.

This project began when a question emerged in a discussion with a colleague on writing drama: What is the role of emotion in determining the shape of drama? I realized that this issue is always present but most difficult to address, for myself as a writer as well as for my students. It led me to examine not only the way emotion works in drama but its role in the life of the writer.

Ordinary life is anything but ordinary; it is filled with conflict and surprise. The power of drama is its ability to tell a story of personal conflict that connects to the narratives of every member of the audience. Most writers agree with this simple statement about life and drama. Why, then, is it so hard to write dramatic narratives that make this emotional connection?

Doesn't drama by its nature create a core experience, an emotional fire in the characters and the audience? Is this fire a matter of luck or talent, more accident than skill? Is this something the writer actually avoids, for whatever reason, instead of pursuing? Does the writer seek it but not understand how it works? Can this difficulty be described and presented in a way that will help the writer to sustain the work? Most important, how are writing—the drama—and the writer at once propelled and shaped by the force of what I call throughout this book emotional form?

This is not a how-to book that applies some jujitsu to the writing task that is supposed to fix technical problems. This is a book about one way to think about, and enter into, the central shaping force of drama: the emotions that fuel the writer's initial interest in the subject, the effort to bring the audience into an awareness of this fuel and how it shapes the narrative arc. Technique alone won't bring the writer any closer to creating powerful work.

The dramatic writer is an arsonist who takes the tangled pieces of what is known and sets them ablaze to reveal what is at once deeply felt and unknown. Learn about this fire, where to seek it and how to connect to it without burning up yourself or your work. This fire of emotion does not arise from words alone, it must combine with lived experience to make meaning. Experience can devastate, heal, challenge, and set free. Writers desire, like audiences, to understand themselves through the liberating prism of imagined action and revealed emotion that drama uniquely allows. Writing in recognition of this self-revelation is the fundamental task of dramatic writing. Passion, intensity, insight, and discovery are not the exclusive possession of long experience; they arise from the pit where the fire burns.

Exploring the process of emotional form draws on a cross-section of theory about drama and fiction, together with the understandings of behavior gained from psychoanalytic practice and theory. As an audience, what do we want to know? We are not satisfied with ideas, intellectual opinions on the nature of man, or moral prescriptions. We want to know why we do what we do. Anyone who has survived childhood knows that being smart, privileged, beautiful, or strong confers no predictable advantage in answering this question. Psychoanalysis and literature are two activities that continuously try. And it is why audiences turn to art in the first place.

This book proposes that emotion is the organizing force of plot, not a by-product. The writer in the act of writing relies upon experience of the world, of self-knowledge applied to an understanding of character, feeling, language, action, and, crucially, an imagined world. These tumble together into a writer's working practice of dramatic structure. The focus on emotional form as framing dramatic structure blends literary and psychoanalytic perspectives. Why psychoanalytic theory? Aren't Sigmund Freud and company old school? Consider how George Lakoff, a linguist, and Mark Johnson, a philosopher, apply cognitive science to what it means to be human:

> Conscious thought is the tip of an enormous iceberg. It is the rule of thumb among cognitive scientists that unconscious thought is 95 percent of all thought—and that may be a serious underestimate. Moreover, the 95 percent below the surface of conscious awareness shapes and structures all conscious thought. . . . Our unconscious conceptual system functions like a "hidden hand" that shapes how we conceptualize all aspects of experience. (13)

Every play is the result of the workings of deep structure, a hidden hand that supports and drives the visible activity of language, character, and action. This deep structure is within the writer, the play, and the audience. Emotional form forges a connection between these structures. The writer voices the desires that break through the veneer of appearances and falsehood when convention, culture, and self-preservation can no longer contain them. This is the work of the writer in touch with the vital energy of emotional form.

A writer is like an explorer with a compass within a great tangled forest that lures us by its sheer, impenetrable size. She chooses a place to enter arbitrarily and plunges in, seeking a high point from which to see more clearly. Like those who searched for the source of the Nile, writers are true believers who think that if they follow a path far enough and deep enough, they will find the source. The one question that haunts every mile of this journey is, What does it mean to be human? The writer is obsessed, not because she thinks she will finally answer that age-old question but because she seeks to make life more vivid, more meaningful, by engaging what continually tests the reach of mind and imagination.

An argument breaks out between two writers in Christopher Shinn's play *What Didn't Happen*. He is asking what we are connected to when we write: ourselves or the world. Or, what is the point of the journey toward the headwaters?

PETER: *(To Elaine.)*: I merely suggested that David write about his own life. His own concerns. So I said he's smarter, more interesting than his books, that's not a criticism—

. . . .

DAVE: God this shit turns you on!
PETER: What turns you on? . . .

. . . .

DAVE: A novel that confronts a wide range of personalities and dilemmas, and I'm *sorry* if you're not interested in certain cultures, in conflicts of survival that don't "touch" you—
PETER: They don't "touch" you either!

. . . .

PETER: The only difference between you and me is that I don't believe the definition of an upper-middle-class person is "someone to whom nothing significant can happen." What do you honestly have to say about those communities you know merely from your trips to the bodega on 121st street? Why *won't* you write about where you live?
DAVE: *(With gravity and feeling.)* I do. This is where I live. Extending into new frontiers, imagination and empathy as one, for if we can't imagine another—if all we can imagine is what we can see—
PETER: —But you can't get rid of yourself in the process, for it's through your self, your very *life*, that you can see it all! (*Beat.*) That's why you're having trouble with the novel. (177–79)

Practice: Everyday Tools

A journal is a tool. Who doesn't have some trouble opening the door to their own experience so it serves their writing? As you pack for the journey into this wilderness, ask what tools point to the path of emotional form. This is certainly one of the reasons writers keep personal journals and why they write every day, without fail. It is a discipline that combines observation, reflection, confession, drudgery, rage, what if, why not, and what do I feel about that. Journals become incubators of script ideas, a way of drawing out a dialogue and a thread of the unconscious on a something that wants to turn into a play. Play ideas can outgrow the journal and move to a wall, a map of your thoughts in a web of pictures, text, diagrams, sounds, and what ifs.

A dream journal is another tool.

Psychological research tells us that if we don't dream at night, we will go insane. Rosalind Cartwright tells us we dream in a kind of dramatic form: launching a dramatic issue or theme in the first of our night's REM episodes and proceeding to work the theme toward some resolution through several acts or episodes of REM sleep during the night.

> Any group of dreams collected on one laboratory night from the same person makes such a coherent statement that it is hard to entertain the idea that these are random events. The dreams of a night constitute a body of thought in which each has meaning singly; but more important, they form an interrelated whole. As a group, they reflect the dreamer's personal responses to waking life and relate these responses to the remembered past and to the hopes and fears of the future. What is more, they do this regularly each night throughout the life span. (129)

So we as dreamers are writing plays about ourselves each night. Perhaps we should try to read them! Untangling a dream, which has a hidden shape and meaning, is not so different than untangling the threads of our writing. Having a rhythm and a process for writing is no less important. Writing plays, like understanding dreams, is a process that engages recalling and interpreting memories, feelings, and actions. It takes time and effort to move through the layers of memory and resistance to find a story and its promise.

A tool that can reveal hidden material is a writer's inventory. I include it here to make clear the terrain I believe the writer must struggle to know. Nobody else need read it.

The Writers Inventory

I. Memory inventory—describe the following:
- A. Earliest memory
- B. Another very early memory
- C. Earliest memory in which your mother is central
- D. Earliest memory in which your father is central
- E. Happiest memory ever
- F. Saddest memory
- G. Most tender memory
- H. Most embarrassing or humiliating memory
- I. The first time you felt real fear

II. Descriptions—using at least 500 words each:
- A. Describe yourself
- B. Describe your mother (or surrogate)
- C. Describe your father (or surrogate)
- D. Describe the person to whom you are closest

III. Illness

Describe any serious illness or operation that you have had in your life and any current illness or chronic condition.
Describe the age at which you were ill and any impact you think the illness may have had on your life.
IV. Separations
Write what you can remember about significant separations in your life. Include any of the following that apply and any others that you remember. Note the approximate age at which each occurred. Tell what you can remember about your reactions to each of the separations.
A. Leaving home for your first schooling
B. Leaving home to go to camp
C. Death of each person who was important to you
D. Leaving home to move into your first independent dwelling
E. Leaving home to be married or to form a partnership
F. Leaving home for college or work or armed service
G. Separations from a spouse or children
H. Divorce
V. Dreams
Make notes for at least six dreams. Try to write the dream down right after you wake up or soon thereafter. Describe the feeling or emotional state that predominated in the dream.
VI. Jokes
Write two jokes that you have heard recently that you liked. Write down two jokes that you remember from childhood. Describe your reactions to them in childhood.
VII. Name the three traits or things about yourself that you like. Name the three traits or things about yourself that you don't like. For what would you most like to be remembered?
VIII. Imagine your future
List in chronological order ten important events that you think will probably occur in your life.
IX. Undoing the past . . . if you had it all to do over again
List six things that you have done in your life that you would most like to undo. Tell why for each one. The reasons need not be elaborate.
X. Focus on your body
A. Which is the part of your body with which you are most pleased? Why?
B. Which is the part of your body with which you are most displeased? Why?
C. What would you change about your body?

D. What part of your body has been the source of greatest pain or suffering? Why?
E. Is there any part of your body for which you have or ever had a name or nickname? If so, which one? Do you still use the nickname for a part of your body? Under which circumstances? At what age did you first remember having a name for a part of your body?

The inventory assumes we hide things from ourselves. It assumes we need a strong push to dive into this hidden well because our need for defenses lets us float on top of these waters, not looking too deeply into what's below. If the writer can't take us, the audience, below the surface of these waters, why do we need her at all? There are a few things like pleasure, entertainment, delight, and surprise the writer is also good for.

Rescue for the Lost

One friend of the bushwhacking playwright is theory. What was the first thing the Greeks did after inventing our subject? They created a theory about it. Theory rescues the lost. It can even serve as a means of organizing, inspiring, and mapping a path through the thickets. Psychology is a theory that creates a map of character and of the expression of inner and outer conflict and connects these to emotional realities that may posses permanent meanings.

All our actions are enmeshed in who and what we are and whom and what we love. The life of every character is created from a primal connection to others and how that constrains or frees them to act in the world. Conflict is not acquired like fish at the market. All characters come onto the scene defined by their inner conflicts. Conflict creates the animated presence of character that is made of the eternal struggle between forces below the neck: wishes, desires, threats, dreams, and appetite, as well as those above the neck: conscience, language, denial, routine, and judgment. The balance between these forces is maintained by compromise and practiced defenses. We create ongoing compromises in our behavior that are coupled with our conflicted emotions about the world below the neck. When these compromises fail or become intolerable to the character or others, you have the material of drama.

There is no escape from examining in some depth the place a writer can't avoid and sometimes dreads—endings. Beginnings have as much to do with igniting what is meaningful and alive in the writer as they do with giving life to the character. We all experience resistance to beginning, usually from fear that we cannot fill the blank page. Imagination provides a way of searching through the attic of our minds, testing images, ideas, and feelings until we find firm footing in a world that compels our discovery. Like any newborn, a beginning creates rising expectations, ready to be tested by experience. Where am I going? Why am I going there? What do I want?

Writers, readers, and theorists of narrative all refer to the idea that the end is in the beginning. They mean that once we know a story's end, we can find it embedded in the characters and situation of the beginning. There may be a margin for error, but we believe they are joined in ways that can't be separated without killing the patient. The folly that unleashes King Lear's devastation lives in the question he asks in the beginning:

> . . . Tell me, my daughters,
> Since now we will divest us both of rule,
> Interest of territory, cares of state,
> Which of you shall we say doth love us most?
> That we our largest bounty may extend
> Where nature doth with merit challenge. (1.1.44–49)

Not only are motive and folly joined but also there is a "how" to their joining, like a genetic code of plot and narrative. Particular to each play or narrative is an emotional form embedded in the central character's whole being, his language, thought, and behavior that shapes the movement toward the end.

We have Aristotle to thank for one of the most basic descriptions of a drama as an "imitation of an action which is complete and whole. . . . 'Whole' is that which has beginning, middle and end" (Else, *Aristotle:* Poetics 30). Both theory and our experience tell us that endings determine meaning.

In psychoanalysis, the patient works to understand how the past connects to the trouble of the present. This is a recognition that the past is reconstituted in the present, in the person's significant relationships. This understanding does not come easily but is developed over time with the analyst in a kind of reenactment of the threats of the past. So, too, in drama. The middle of the play is a crucible of pressure and resistance where the writer works for the insights that will break through to an end and to meaning. A writer can build internal resistance to the threats embedded in the narrative, creating a barrier to the end. The writer focuses on the work of discovery, finding the threats embedded in the character's emotional barriers that erect a defense against change and are the clue to the experience that can bring new knowledge and recognition. The end.

A Doll's Threat

Nora in Henrik Ibsen's *Doll's House* is an example of the impact of threat on character and the layered meaning it can create. Nora is a character who, because of the power of threat, cannot reveal a persistent desire. The play shows what happens when containment of the threat and the deep wish it suppresses fails. To change a character's denial and concealment requires new experience and new knowledge, a different relationship to the past and to the present. If loss anchors the beginning terrain of emotional form, new experience and knowledge anchor the ending terrain. It is the classic architecture of profound character change and discovery where the lives of the characters are remade at the end.

Nora's behavior with her husband, Torvald Helmer, is a replay of her behavior with her father, including the way she negotiated her father's love. She is two Noras. One Nora allows Torvald to treat her like a child who needs his guidance and permission. In the scene with her friend Mrs. Linde, the other Nora is revealed, the capable Nora, who saves Torvald's health by securing a bank loan and who takes him to a climate where he can recover. There is a deep threat in Nora's fear of revealing the source of the borrowed money to Torvald, who believes it was a gift from her father. We know Krogstad, who works for Torvald, is the man who helped her, and we know she forged her father's signature on the loan three days after he died. Krogstad's knowledge embodies the threat of revealing the two Noras by the secret of the loan.

The Nora who took the risk to borrow the money for her husband's health is not the Nora her husband is in love with. If the other Nora, whom Torvald does not know or love, has a wish for a love who will be her protector and take the blame if her secret is found out, who is that figure of her desire on whom she pins the hope, "Something glorious is going to happen" (68)? Who was Nora saving when she borrowed the money? What desire is concealed in the act of taking the loan? Everything about the loan brings together her father and Torvald, who says of people who commit lies, "I honestly feel sick, sick to my stomach, in the presence of such people" (40). Did she misdate the loan because she was distracted by Torvald's sickness, or did she wish to be discovered?

One way to look at the threat is to see in it the desire to make her father love her. Her boldness in taking the loan is a seduction. She ceases to perform the girl and acts the woman. But she fears these actions. On one level, they will be seen as "unwomanly" but on a deeper level as forbidden. They will result in the loss of the one she loves. She denies this threat by her fantasy that the act will be the thing that keeps and secures that love. She has acted like a man, taken risks in the world, borrowed money like a man, which will make her father love her as she really is. She wants to be loved as more than the girl who is kept like a doll. If women are loved as dolls kept from reality, true love must be reserved for the actions that men take.

In the final scene, Nora recognizes the similarity between the way she behaved with her father and with her husband. She sees that even though her father treated her as an object to be controlled, played with, and dismissed as morally inferior, she wished for a different love. Nora defines the "something glorious" to Torvald as an act that couldn't be taken back or changed no matter what she does.

NORA: When that had happened, I believed with such utter certainty that you would step forward, you would take the blame, you would say, "I am the guilty one."

HELMER: Nora—

NORA: You believe I would never have allowed such a sacrifice from you. No, of course not. But would what I have to say count against what you had to say? That was the glorious thing I hoped for and feared. And to stop that happening I wanted to end my life. (103)

She is not describing the mutual love of adults, but the protective love of a parent. She describes an act that transgresses on the adult's world as a theft of its love without consequences. At the heart of this something glorious is the seductive wish to be possessed by her father, which is the source of her disturbance. Thus, she considers suicide to prevent it and tells Mrs. Linde that it is "frightening," and "It can't happen, not for anything in the world" (68). Torvald's tirade rips the mask from her wish, she recognizes the truth of her desire and thus the impossibility of this relationship. In her rush to escape this now shameful place, this transforming realization separates her even from her children: "I realized I'd lived with a stranger for eight years and that I'd borne him three children—I can't bear to think of it. It tears me to pieces" (104).

Stunned by her recognition, she rejects Torvald, as if he were tainted. There must be no contact. She will take nothing from the house that belongs to him. He cannot write her, give her money, nothing. She must remove the symbol of her marriage, her ring, and he must remove his. She flees without seeing her children as if she and they are touched with incest. Nora is a courageous figure paying the price for her insistence that life should be about something greater, "That our marriage could become a life together" (106). Her knowledge makes her a tragic figure, an echo of the Greek stage. The famous door bangs shut. Nora hurtles into exile, fleeing the wish she consummated with Torvald that now severs her from the world she knew. This reading of the play shows how threat enters into every aspect of a character's ability to act and how the desire underlying the threat becomes the emotional linchpin of the ending.

An evident principle will confront the writer: drama often uses a central character to create the narrative core of a play, just as the secondary characters support it. Indispensable as they are, Polonius's and Ophelia's stories are secondary to Hamlet's. It is their connection to the central character's story that explains their presence in the play; otherwise, there is no need for them at all. Sam is only in *"MASTER HAROLD" . . . and the boys* because he is indispensable to Hally's story. Goldberg is only in *The Birthday Party* because it is Stanley's story. As vital as each is to the whole, their stories and their fates are secondary. Polonius may well have had his own play if Shakespeare had believed he could carry the weight of being the central character, but Shakespeare put Polonius behind that curtain for one reason only: to advance Hamlet's story. The demand for a central character sits in the writer's path like a troll who if you appear without one must be convinced that you've created an equivalent by other means before it will let you pass.

Practice: The Troll's Test

There is a reason theaters ask to see fifteen or so pages of a play before asking for the rest. When you send in those pages, you are taking a test: Does the play have an engine that pulls the events toward a future that is worth the journey? Has the writer turned the ignition and started that engine in these first pages? Has something happened that complicates the future of a character, and do we care? If you can't mark the moment you think this ignition fires, no one else will see it either. A character has a desire that pulls us toward a reckoning. We see enough of that desire to know it is alive in the way a gathering storm moves toward us. If you don't care about getting past the troll, if you haven't made something happen that irrevocably changes or will change the world of the play, the troll will pull you and your play into the swamp.

Who's Paying Attention

You start to write a play. You have barely finished choosing the time and place when you realize there is the audience that comes, to listen, laugh, cry, be bored or thrilled. What good is it to know the power and sweep of emotion that brings characters to renewal or devastation, to have the discipline of the writer and the bank account of a chimney sweep if no one shows up to buy a ticket?

From the Greeks of the sixth century B.C.E., the long story of drama in the West always includes the audience. The audience is never to be taken for granted. What do we know or need to know about what takes place between an audience and the performance of a drama? There is, of course, the other problem: the aspiring writer usually is adrift, stuck in an enervating loop between creation and developmental readings that never leads to an actual audience, at an actual theater, of an actual performance of the writer's play. In the space between that actual audience and the flesh-and-blood performers is a psychological and emotional nervous system that links the writer, the text, the players, and the audience.

Plot? Blame the Greeks for deciding that the subject of tragedy was the loss, suffering, and humiliation of the tragic hero, what they called *pathos*. The Greeks make tragic pathos part of the DNA of emotional form. The Greeks' astonishing cultural invention was to focus not on great deeds or adventures but on the hero's catastrophe. They invented a narrative structure made of a character's blindness, discovery, disaster, and loss, leading to self-knowledge and meaning. Aristotle thought this was a big deal, big enough to write the *Poetics*.

The Greeks also gave us catharsis. Without it, we couldn't write about the emotionally complex, dangerous, and instinctual side of human life. Society constructs powerful systems of judgment and punishment for the destructive and transgressive acts of human behavior. Tragedy opened the door on pariah behavior such as murder within families, still a favorite crime statistic. For drama to enter this part of the human experience, the writer had to separate the action of a character from a base intention to commit the act. Otherwise, the character inspires nothing but contempt. This separation of the character's intention, a cleansing of the character's knowledge of his action, allows the audience to experience pity and fear and is the very mechanism of catharsis.

We can't talk about the process of writing without looking at the thing itself. We can't unpack the elements of emotional form without looking at examples so readers can judge for themselves the reality of the claim. Several plays as case studies show the different aspects of emotional form. Writing and reading go together. The works chosen become an open laboratory where the play can be poked, dismantled, and peered into. This is a place where we can ask, How is it done, or how did this writer do it? Can we see the path of emotional form ripped out of the ordinary, things broken and trampled underfoot, hidden, bloodied, or marked with diversions and feints?

What Is This Good For?

I once participated in a month-long workshop by Peter Schumann of Bread and Puppet Theatre. One project we created was a staging of Franz Kafka's short story *Josephine and the Mouse Singer.* The title Peter gave to this performance was *What Is Art and What Is It Good For*? Because it was a workshop, he indulged us in a process where he invited us to show how we would adapt the story for performance. Some of us entertained, for a brief time, the illusion of our adaptations winning the day. But as soon as we were in the grip of Peter's creative process, we realized that his years of practice and his process of visualizing the emotional beats of the work were like a poet's vision that would consume the narrative of Kafka's story in ways we couldn't imagine or consider. We all quickly yielded to Peter's process and through it allowed ourselves to feel our way through his recreation of Kafka's work. When I thought about why he chose his title, I realized that this question is answered solely in the doing of it: for the artist, in sustaining the effort of creation; for the audience, in sustaining its role as essential witness. So the answer involves what occurs over time, what is deeply felt that burns in the artist, something that isn't tidied up and satisfied by the application of technique or surefire rules. If this book is of any use, it will be as a wind to drive the fire that burns in the writer, to show the power and ferocious humanity that is at the center of the writer's work. Taking that journey is the only way to answer the questions, What is art, and what is it good for?

1. The Seeds of Emotional Form

> Do you know what this is? It's a curse. I can feel it. It's invisible but it's there. It's always there. It comes onto us like nighttime. Every day I can feel it. Every day I can see it coming. And it always comes. Repeats itself. It comes even when you do everything to stop it from coming. Even when you try to change it. And it goes back. Deep.
>
> —Sam Shepard, *Curse of the Starving Class*

What Dionysus Has to Do with It

Perhaps it is because I came of age in the sixties that I don't consider Dionysus simply a quaint antiquarian construct. I saw it in the streets of Berkeley, I felt it in myself: the pull to run to the mountain to know what wasn't taught in the classroom, to call the god forth, to become one, to let the body know what the intellect cannot. The streets south of campus were littered with refugees from a middle-class America whose vision of security and success totally rejected the Dionysian. I have been somewhat like Pentheus, drawn to the rites on the mountain but fearful. I've been a creature of reason who has tried to know the world beyond reason through art. This awareness is a product of reading, of travel, of event, of failure, and of skepticism. This is the same but different for anyone who is a writer. Everyone has experience, but the writer demands awareness.

Defenders of order regard the writer as a threat, as a disruptive, dangerous, and seductive voice. This is not Greek to us. We know it from the twentieth century's experiments with totalitarianism, our own nation's experience with battling "un-American activities," and the demagoguery of the contemporary "culture wars" over values. Dramatic writing has the fortune of having a patron saint. That figure is no saint by contemporary standards, yet the Greeks considered him the god of the theater, the god of transformation, transgression of boundaries, ecstatic joy, profound reverence, blood, and death. The awareness of the undeniable power of Dionysus in human nature was rekindled by one of the great conjurers of modernism, Friedrich Nietzsche.

The runaway kids on the sidewalks of Telegraph Avenue in Berkeley were not there out of curiosity or some ordinary family dispute; they were joining an exodus to the mountain to experience a dance, a way of seeing the invisible in their early lives. I see the act of dramatic writing as evoking Dionysus or what the Greeks pointed to by evoking his name. The power of emotional form draws upon our culture's recognition that human experience grows out of conscious and unconscious forces that we deny at our peril. The writer cannot make Pentheus's mistake and flee or bully the expression of these forces in our lives, the expression of a profound source of our vitality and our knowledge of death.

Consider the physicality and surprise that words inhabit. A writer's ritual practice might involve a conjuring, a prayer, a curse, a supplication, a rage, a mock, a put-down, a song, a whispered desire, or a secret. In her essay "Elements of Style," Suzan-Lori Parks reminds us that words are attached to the body.

> Language is a physical act. It's something which involves your entire body—not just your head. Words are spells which an actor consumes and digests—and through digesting creates a performance on stage. Each word is configured to give the actor a clue to their physical life. Look at the difference between "the" and "thuh." The "uh" requires the actor to employ a different physical, emotional, vocal attack. (11, 12)

What does a writer need to know about Dionysus, the god of tragedy and comedy? All Athenian plays were performed as part of festivals that celebrated Dionysus. Who is this god of the theater? Well, resurrection was one of Dionysus's traits when he was reborn from the thigh of his father, Zeus, after a lightning bolt blasted his human mother, Semele. He also has two sides to his nature, as shown by the different names for him in Euripides' *Bacchae*: "He is Bacchus, Iacchus, and Evius—all names that evoke the joy of worshiping this god of peace and wine and dancing. He is also Bromius, the Thunderer, born in a blast of lightning, bringing terror against his enemies" (x).

Dionysus is bound up with our connection to nature, our connection to our mortal bodies in dance and words and song, a suspension of daily order, a blurring or shedding of individuality, a joining with others. Those who know him experience peace and joy. He is also bound to a frenzy of the blood, an intimacy with death.

Losing One's Mind to Find It: A Writer's Task?

The *Bacchae* presents one of the most common features of the myth of Dionysus, the resistance to his worship and the consequences of resistance. Resistance is a key feature of the story of Dionysus, although the Greeks worshiped Dionysus from earliest times (*Bacchae*, x). In Euripides' play, Dionysus has come to Thebes, where he was born of a union between a human mother and Zeus, to punish his mother's sisters for denying the divinity of his birth. He has come with a chorus of Asian Bacchantes, his initiates and worshippers. Dionysus incites Agave, the mother of Pentheus, the young King of Thebes, to lead all the women of Thebes to abandon their homes so they can go to the mountain to worship Dionysus. King Pentheus demands an end to this disruptive worship and demands the women return home. He believes the women are engaging in sexual orgies on the mountain and that the rites threaten the order of his city.

Dionysus, either by altering Pentheus's perception or by drawing on Pentheus's inner wish, persuades him to dress as a woman to spy on the rites. Doesn't he want to see for himself their secret rites? Dionysus leads him to the mountain, sets him on the tip of a pine tree, and then makes Pentheus's presence known to the women. He tells the women he has brought the one who has ridiculed the worship: "Now you must pay him back." The women tear the pine tree from the earth "while the god breathed madness in them." The messenger tells what next happens to Pentheus:

> His mother was the first at the killing. She was priestess,
> And she rushed to attack him. He tore off his headband
> in hopes she would recognize him, not kill him.
> He reached out to her cheek, miserable Agave's,
> and said, "I am yours, Mother, your child Pentheus."
>
> . . . .
>
> She was possessed by Bacchus and did not believe him.
>
> . . . .
>
> The body is spread around: one piece by a rugged
> cliff, another deep in the woods under heavy foliage,
> impossible to find. His head—this is horrible—
> it turned out that his mother took it in her hands. (45–46)

Agave, his mother, returns to town proudly bearing the head of her son. She believes it is the head of a mountain lion until her father tells her the head she is holding belongs to the broken corpse of her son. Paul Woodruff, the translator, says of the ritual element of the play:

> That paradox of losing one's mind in order to gain it is fundamental to Dionysiac religion, even though celebrants evidently do not use words for madness (mania) of themselves. . . . The wisdom of initiation is a serene acceptance that comes through letting go, an acceptance

> achieved through the frenzy of initiation. Such wisdom is totally incompatible with the wisdom of intellectuals such as Tiresias in this play, who have no intention of losing their wits—who try, indeed, to use their wits for exercising control over others. (xv)

Walking on Fire

In the act of writing, the writer engages the same forces attached to Dionysus: transformation, disguise, reality and illusion, resistance, the divine and human, joy, reverence, and death. In the creative act, the writer seeks to voice both his knowledge of the resistance of a Pentheus who doesn't deserve his destruction, as well as a knowledge of the "madness" of Agave, blinded by the mysteries of her own life force.

We are not Greeks of the fifth century, but we are inheritors of an art form that was born in the emotional knowledge of the Dionysian in human experience. Woodruff offers this description of Dionysus.

> He does not merely cross boundaries, he blurs and confounds them, makes nonsense of the lines between Greek and foreign, between female and male, between powerful and weak, between savage and civilized. . . . We might say, then, that Dionysus appears mysterious because he is mysterious, because it is his special role to undermine the boundaries set by human culture. (xl)

The writer is both a conservative who openly presents his work for viewing and understanding as a force for civic preservation and a disruptive force that shows the stories of human action that put at risk the boundaries between good and evil, human and inhuman, love and hate, male and female, chaos and order, fear and freedom, excess and moderation, aggression and tolerance, isolation and mutuality, safety and recklessness, narcissism and conscience. When the writer walks into these fires, there is always risk: of being burned, of resisting and seeing the body of the play disintegrate, even of encountering the dead. If this fire is Dionysus, then the art of the writer is the art of evoking his presence.

Writing Practice and Emotional Form

A new work may be as close as writers get to a religious experience. We know some of the signs: a taste for poverty, visions buzzing in the head, characters talking in tongues, and the stamina for wandering in the desert. The signs may test faith, but the acts of "worship," of shaping language in a public space, renew the calling.

A consensus among many of those who write about playwriting is at once convincing and unsettling. On one hand is general agreement about theory. Everyone points to the interconnected principles of character, conflict, structure, story, and plot. The writer brings the personal and internal frame of reference that launches and completes the shaping events of the narrative. The writer brings her own story, a past and a self who lives in time and in the currents of art, of history, of politics. At the same time, she embraces the paradoxes between ways of knowing, between the physical and the spiritual.

The writer's practice can be further divided into at least three parts: (1) the internal world, the web of act, word, dream, and body; (2) the external world, the web of time, other people, place, and events; and (3) a question, "What does Dionysus have to do with it?" The writer has a character formed of loss and conflicts from a personal past. The writer creates a construct of the outside world out of the trash of cultural behavior, the architecture of ideas, the arrangements of power, and judgments on what is good and just. The writer always deals with some version of Dionysus: the mysteries of our experience of death and spirituality.

The writer's drive is a dynamic connected to the impact of lived experience: intellectual, emotional, political, and the place of a moral compass in life's meaningful relationships. To create a character is to create an imagined life. There is no life without choice, desire, consequences, and love. The writer's own life is not put on the shelf while she creates the imagined life on the page; it is the source of that imagined life the writer works to shape into a meaning. The connection between the real and imagined life, the place where they profoundly connect, is through those intersections of plot and narrative where emotional form holds sway.

Where can we get this thing called emotional form? It is called by other names, such as, spirit, fate, destiny, luck, catastrophe, desire, will, and transformation. In defining emotional form, I take my cue from the psychoanalytic understanding of human behavior. In life, emotional form is the shape of a person's experience drawn by the internal forces of conflict formed in childhood. Our experience of loss creates the structure of character that impacts our choices and our behaviors, knowing and unknowing. It determines the force, presence, and tone of a person acting in the world and especially with those they care about. The following is an example from life that shows the relationship between a conflict (a condition that may cause misery) and the event of change. It shows that knowledge and feeling are the chemicals that mix in emotional form. This is a story about Julia that comes from a psychologist's office.

Julia comes to a treatment center seeking help for an eating disorder. When she begins group therapy, she describes how she is estranged from her father and how that has affected her relationship to her whole family. When she goes home for holidays, she can barely force herself to listen as her siblings talk about their lives. She tells the group she is estranged because her father has never shared with her his experiences in a Nazi concentration camp, although he has shared them with her siblings.

One special technique of this group is that a member who has an insight into another member's true, unnamable feelings is permitted to stand behind that person, put a hand on that person's shoulder and speak for that person. Thus, the therapist has given the patients the writer's job: to voice the emotional form underlying another's resistant language.

The therapy group has scheduled special days for parents and significant others to join the session, and Julia's father is present on one such day. The group immediately wants to know why he didn't tell Julia about his experiences. Doesn't he realize that this makes her feel cut off from him? The father is dumbfounded by this question. He says the distance between them also disturbs him. Then he protests that he did in fact tell her about his past in the concentration camp.

He turns to Julia and asks, "Didn't I tell you how the soldiers came to our synagogue in Prague. When they herded us outside, my father tried to protect me from one of the soldiers. The soldier knocked my father down. He then struck his head with his rifle butt and bashed his brains out?"

Julia says, "Yes, you said this, but you didn't really describe what this was like."

Her father says, "And didn't I tell you that when I was in the camp, both the Nazi guards and the collaborators in our barracks repeatedly raped me?"

Julia says, "Yes, but you didn't really help me to understand what that was like."

Her father says, "Didn't I tell you how one day I walked around a building and saw a pile of bodies in which I saw my mother's face? And when I ran toward her, the soldiers knocked me down? And how I kept getting up and trying to reach her, and each time I tried, they knocked me down until I passed out?"

Julia says, "Yes, but you never told me what that felt like."

Everyone in the group began to weep, except Julia. She was frozen in her repetitive response to her father. A member of the group stood and walked behind Julia and put his hand on her shoulder so he could speak to her father as Julia.

That person said, "I know you told me these things happened, but it was too painful to accept. I was overwhelmed. I couldn't stand the pain of knowing you'd suffered so horribly. I love you too much." Julia burst into tears at these words. Her father suddenly realized that her distance and her isolation had been out of her love for him. Julia embraced her father. The group, moved by this sudden discovery, began to say the Kaddish.

Julia couldn't respond to the knowledge she already had and so denied that she had heard it. New experience makes knowledge. It is the human mechanism of change breaking open a character's hidden and conflicted feelings. Julia's recognition within the group made her feelings visible to her, uncovering the source of her denial. The discovery of her denial is knowledge that marks an end to the arc of an emotional form. The chain of events from denial to discovery creates a narrative map of Julia's character. Such behavior involves the surprise that what seems like one thing in a character is actually the opposite. Julia's estrangement was not out of coldness or hostility but out of her love. The discovery assumes a connection of two elements, feeling and knowledge. We are used to hearing that a play can create its own rules and that the writer must abide by these rules. This coherence of imagination requires that the rules the writer creates are not contradictory or abandoned halfway through. This expectation rests on a metarule formed in our experience of our own actual emotional lives: change contains the dynamic relationship in which knowledge and feeling connect or disconnect through the arc of experience. Every dramatic structure must address this metarule regardless of the rules of invention.

In drama, emotional form is the internal emotional structure, or plot, the writer gives to a narrative. It is made from the character's created life, knowing and unknowing, experiences of transformation, loss, yearning, and denial. We experience emotional form through characters and action—who does what to whom, when, and how. Emotional form is the life force in a play, marking the dramatic world through desire and conflict and cutting a way through silence and dialogue to what is essential to the presence of dimensional life. A play doesn't explain its emotional form. It reveals it by what it does with its characters and to the audience. The understanding that comes from emotional form is not the result of a formula, any more than psychoanalytic understanding is. Understanding is ignited by the unrelenting course of events that reveals the path a character takes to knowledge of who they are.

A writer has experience, but this is more active and complex than simply being acted upon by time and events. The writer experiences the same desires, needs, losses, and hopes as others, even though the writer is called to know these things by the methods of art. It is no surprise that the writer is a person, but what matters is the writer's willingness to look at what is available through feelings, imagination, and a courageous openness to what is ugly but beautiful, desirable but destructive, essential yet frightening, foolish but appropriate, knowable but evil.

Yes, in the beginning was the word. It contains the wish, the desire, and, hence, the act. The word also contains the resistance to the act, if we are to believe the symmetry of creation. This resistance is external and internal, answerable to law and conscience. Desire is not bound by a world of order and rules but is held in a tense compromise by the conflicts that define every individual. Those individuals without such conflicts are psychopaths, and it is unlikely they are submitting work to their local theaters.

What is the material of these conflicts? Pain, loss, failed and successful relationships, fear, excess, aggression, self-aggrandizement, lies, physicality, manipulation, panic, invention, wit, music, obsession, love: all things the writer needs to know. This means you know more than you think. The knowing of feelings associated with our experience lies in a conflicted state within us, an elusive and constant mystery that can yield to the writer's honest discipline.

When we tell a story, it is because some aspect of our experience is pressing hard on us to give it voice and meaning. This meaning can be revised and made visible, but it must be found. However, one story is not as good as another. The storyteller will stamp an emotional imprint on the desire that initiated the story and upon the events of the narrative. Call it emotional form.

Athol Fugard: *"MASTER HAROLD" . . . and the boys*

Fugard's play demonstrates the explosive role of change when ignorance and desire encounter truth. The structure of emotional change alters this play from an initial exercise in lively talk in a South African tearoom to a drama of race and forbidden love. We know from Fugard's notes about this play that it is an example of the connective tissue between the writer's personal feelings and the new life and shape they become in the created work. Fugard says his play comes from his own childhood and his relationship to the real Sam. He describes how as a boy he met Sam. As he rode his bicycle passed this black man whom he knew and saw daily, he spat on him. Years later the man, the writer, devises a drama that untangles the conflicted pieces in this shameful act of the child.

> Can't remember now what precipitated it, but one day there was a rare quarrel between Sam and myself. In a truculent silence we closed the café, Sam set off home to New Brighton on foot and I followed a few minutes later on my bike. I saw him walking ahead of me and, coming out of a spasm of acute loneliness, as I rode up behind him I called his name, he turned in mid-stride to look back and, as I cycled past, I spate in his face. Don't suppose I will ever deal with the shame that overwhelmed me the second after I had done that. (*Notebooks*, 26)

Fugard's play begins on a rainy afternoon in a tearoom in a South Africa wracked by apartheid. We see three characters: Sam, the older and more worldly of two black men who work in the tearoom; Willy, the younger and more impulsive; and Master Harold, whom Sam calls Hally. He is the white teenage son of the tearoom's proprietors.

Hally has known Sam and Willy all his life. Previous to the tearoom was a boarding house, both businesses run by Hally's mother because his father is an amputee who spends much of his time drinking. We quickly learn that Sam and Hally have a close, obviously familial relationship. After school, Hally comes to the tearoom to do his homework, and Sam helps him, all the while careful to remember his place, a *kaffir* in this viciously segregated society. This avoidance is one way they sidestep the wrenching social conditions that bestow unlimited power to white people and none to blacks. This distorted relationship between a white boy and a black man will not endure the day under the pressure of change that is voicelessly delivered by telephone.

Despite Hally's unconscious white-boy swagger around the two black men, everything about his relationship with Sam appears genial and affectionate. They joke with each other in a way that only people who have known each other for a long time do, softening the bitter reality that exists outside the tearoom. Sam treats Hally with the patience and concern one associates with a father. When Hally arrives on this particular rainy day, they reminisce about the old days at the boardinghouse when Hally was a little boy and spent his time in the servants' room.

Willy is about to enter a ballroom dance competition with his friend Hilda, whom he occasionally "knocks about a bit," and Hally is encouraged to write his homework essay on the subject of black ballroom dance contests. Hally says there should be a point system to penalize couples who collide on the dance floor. The change at the end of the play will contrast cruelly to the hope found in this metaphor.

> There's no collisions out there, Hally. Nobody trips or stumbles or bumps into anybody else. That's what that moment is all about. To be one of those finalists on that dance floor is like . . . like being in a dream about a world in which accidents don't happen. . . . No one knows the steps and there's no music playing. And it doesn't stop with us. The whole world is doing it all the time. . . . People get hurt in all that bumping, and we're sick and tired of it now. It's been going on for too long. Are we never going to get it right? (*"MASTER HAROLD,"* 45–46)

If this day was like all other days, Hally would finish his homework; the men would close the tearoom and go home. Woven into the badinage that accompanies the doing of Hally's homework is the story of Hally's real father. A phone call from his mother informs us that his father will return home from the hospital on this day, and this pins the narrative to an emotional clock toward a change in Hally's conflict. Can he love two fathers, one white and one black?

Hally's feelings for his father are profoundly conflicted. They are conflicted in ways Hally can't admit and that the play will dramatize. Hally wants to love, and to be loved, by his real father. His father is a drunken, abusive racist who believes his son should share his belief in apartheid. He teaches him how to take charge of the "boys" at the tearoom. But it is at the tearoom that Hally finds the love of a man, Sam, who teaches him how to make a kite, play checkers, and write an essay on black ballroom dance contests. In Hally's segregated world, he is not allowed to love this "father" because he's black. But at the same time, he has a son's desire to love his real father, who is white. The play plots an emotional form that drives the character toward having to "choose" between these two "fathers."

Change is a key marker of emotional form. Change is a process drawing on the conflicted forces holding a character's status quo in place. Hally's change begins when his mother calls him with the news of his father's homecoming. Hally furiously attacks his mother for letting this happen, but when his father is put on the phone, Hally shows himself as the son eager to have him home. When Hally hangs up, it is as if both "fathers" are in the room with him. He can no longer keep them separate. In his frustration and rage, he attacks them both. The feelings of his conflicted love and shame for his father are open and vulnerable to the truth.

Hally rips up his "world without collisions" homework that Sam has helped him to write, then he smashes a bottle of brandy he was to take home to his father. He lets loose a stream of venom aimed at his father, making him the crippled spoiler of Sam's world without collisions.

"Nobody knows the steps, there's no music, the cripples are also out there tripping everybody up and trying to get into the act, and it's called the All-Comers-How-to-Make-a-Fuckup-of-Life-Championships" ("*MASTER HAROLD*," 51–52). Sam knows he is going too far and tries to stop him. Sam's efforts to restrain Hally only make him more upset and mean. Finally, Hally chooses the worst of the alternatives he attacks and humiliates Sam, as his father has "educated" him to do. He becomes the racist bully he despises.

> HALLY: You're only a servant in here, and don't forget it. (*Still no response. Hally is trying hard to get one.*) And as far as my father is concerned, all you need to remember is that he is your boss.

Hally tells Sam to call him "Master Harold," a mark of respect that will please his father whom he now defends.

> HALLY: He's got a marvelous sense of humor. Want to know what our favorite joke is? He gives out a big groan, you see, and says, "It's not fair, is it, Hally?" Then I have to ask: "What, chum?" And then he says: "A nigger's arse" . . . and we both have a good laugh. (55)

Hally pushes deeper, claiming he really laughed at the joke and not just to please his father.

Fugard finds the destructive core of Hally's conflict. The emotional form finds an opening in the event of change either to new knowledge—opening Hally's conflict to new understanding—or a closing and a price paid for failing this moment. Sam asks Hally how he knows it's not fair, then drops his pants and shows Hally his "nigger's arse." Sam pulls his trousers up and tells Hally he can go home and tell his father that he was right: it isn't fair. Hally pauses for a moment then, and as Sam passes his chair, he speaks his name. Sam leans closer to hear what the boy has to say. Hally turns and spits in his face. In the collision of feeling and knowledge, Hally cannot contain his confusion and shame at loving two fathers. Sam tries to recover from the collision he worked so hard to avoid and watches Hally shrug into his raincoat and leave. The truth has knocked away the compromise that had made their relationship possible, but now neither knows whether they can ever be together in the same way again.

If you listed the events of the story that make the sequence of scenes in this play, they would not prepare you for the moment when Hally spits in Sam's face. Plot pins the story to an emotional shape, binds it to conflict, change, and consequence. The story tells how Hally comes to the tearoom after school as usual; Sam engages with Hally over his homework lessons; a series of phone calls from Hally's mother informs him his father is returning home from the hospital. Plot threads the knots to Hally's reaction, his conflict bends the narrative to the shape and rush of his feelings. Each phone call opens up the character of Hally, showing more of his conflict, rage and yearning. The emerging force of this conflict grows until it becomes intolerable and Hally strikes against the false balance of his world. The force pushing Hally's character to that moment traces an emotional form that begins when Hally first learns his father will return home, and he is unable to contain his feelings.

Bearings: The Kindest Cuts

So what does this have to do with Dionysus or emotional form? A placid-seeming status quo, a tearoom, a young boy, two older men. What we know at the start is their entwined familiarity, a history between Sam and Hally that extends back to Hally's childhood. We also know the perilous context of their relationship: two black men and a white boy in apartheid South Africa. That sends waves through the surface waters of the tearoom as the natural authority between age and youth is turned on its head by race. This is a play that points us to how emotional form breaks open the status quo so that it is never the same again. We know from the story of Dionysus we will pay for resisting or denying the passions that animate our inner life, that which is at the core of our humanity. What we call our character is a skin laced tight to contain the desires and feelings that press against the comfort of our status quo. The writer, understanding emotional form, uses events like a scissors to snip away the laces binding the truth until it cannot be contained.

Fugard constructs an elegant dramatic box for his character Master Harold. The name of that box is conflict. At the beginning of the play, the space of the box is clean. His father is in the hospital out of sight. Hally has free range with the man who acts like a father but who is not and who is tainted by taboo in this racist world. Everything is contained so they can reminisce, do homework, talk of the world as long as the two fathers remain separate. This lack of conflict is a why we say out of sight, out of mind. Simply, step by step, Fugard snips the laces using the device of the mother's phone calls reporting the progress to his father's imminent return. Each call brings Hally's real father closer and closer to the boxed space of the tearoom. With each call, Hally, like the enraged Pentheus, resists and rails against the rising conflict. The resistance lasts until the final call when it is certain the father will be coming home from the hospital. At that point, the two fathers are in the same emotional space, and all hell breaks loose. The conflict, his love of two fathers that cannot coexist, was always there, only now it cannot be denied or even managed. What happens is ugly, shameful, impossible to retract or pretend it didn't happened. A man who loves him is incited to drop his pants to make a lesson of a crude racist joke, and a boy confused by the fury of his conflict spits in the face of the man he most loves. We know conflict through such emotional markers as the dodge, the defense, aggression, and delusion. Drama is filled with the elaborate dance by bound characters struggling to face their conflicts. Emotional form traces the pattern of their steps lurching toward release and recognition or destruction.

Although the term *conflict* is sometimes viewed as a fusty term of dramatic structure, we as writers are in the same situation as Master Harold. We can pretend it doesn't really matter what we know, or we can boldly try to face what we don't know. But then things will never look the same again. What more is there to learn about conflict? Let's see.

2. *The Fire Hose and the Nozzle*

History is time that won't quit.
—Suzan-Lori Parks, *The Elements of Style*

What you truly know you can go ahead and tell, but what you don't! Hell! You can't even name the name of it.
—Mac Wellman, *The Hyacinth Macaw*

When writers think about conflict, they often start with two sides clashing over some prize, two people arguing, choosing what can easily become a cartoon conflict as in, "He's bad, he's good, bang, slam, see them fight." Conflict without the psychological dimension used by emotional form results in varying techniques of shouting, the pushing and shoving of adversaries. Writers are lured into this choice by the ubiquitous example of sport as a paradigm of conflict in our culture. We can easily fall into the habit of seeing conflict in supposedly objective terms, as a testing ground in which sides are joined, with clear winners and losers at the end. The sport version of conflict is seductive because the act of competing and defeating another produces an emotional charge. To lose arouses feelings of weakness, humiliation, emasculation, and anger, while to win arouses feelings of power, dominance, control, and pleasure. In sport, all of these appear without narrative context or mechanism for resolution. We are familiar with sport programming that supplies narratives taken from athletes' lives that aim to make what is essentially an arbitrary contest more like a drama. Sports drama nearly always portrays the overcoming of adversity to shine on the appointed day. It is fine if sport borrows from drama to make its repetitive conflict more interesting, but it shrinks drama to narrow the definition of its conflict from sport. Our experience tells us that we never defeat, that is, permanently remove, the conflicts of connection and action: they are always with us.

At the beginning, the writer is moving around in a terrain that will lead to a road through an as-yet-unknown landscape. He is circling the character who will fashion this road and determine its destination. And the character's experience is the writer's way of probing into the character and scouting the material of emotional form. You can call this backstory, but what is called backstory often sounds more like sociology casework than the makings of a dramatic narrative. As writers, we scan the world through the eyes of the character, looking for what will propel the character forward. We can imagine other characters and events; we can play what if in a kind of spin the wheel that does not yet explore the central dynamic: the experience of loss and the conflict that determines a character's action.

What Is the Threat?

All drama has conflict, but not all conflict has drama. Conflict moves along a continuum from external to internal, and the heat of the conflict rises with the intensity of the threat. The statements "I'm afraid to love anyone" and "I'm afraid to love because she is black and I'm white and this is Mississippi" pose different threats that completely change the emotional basis of the conflict. The internal conditions the external and vice versa. They become symbiotic as the private goes public. Conflict slips loose the rules of decorum and transgresses the boundaries between allowed and not allowed. The potential for collision is real and inevitable. As creators, we know a story when we feel the bite of time; as audience members, we, too, are bitten and lean forward to watch.

External threats are familiar to us: the dangerous neighborhood you stumble into when lost, the boss who may cost you your job, the religious absolutes you defy, the gun that suddenly appears in the heat of accusation or shame, a sexuality that attracts the enmity of others. Threats arise when a character crosses paths with someone who responds with violent opposition. They come from being put in harm's way due to lack of money or power or both. Most of us learn to live so we can avoid such threats, but drama doesn't seek us out for its characters. The stories single out those who are at imminent risk, and the writer intensifies the threat and gives to the conflict its all-important emotional and moral stakes.

Threat differs from conflict. A threat can be removed at any point and applied to someone else. Conflict is structural. It is embedded in the characters and their stories. Oedipus and his people face the threat of the plague that has fallen on Thebes. Oedipus believes he can remove the threat, by catching the murderer of Laius, who caused the curse and the plague. But the threat can't be removed. Threat is transformed into tragic conflict, as Oedipus is the murderer and the cause. As the conflict becomes internal, structural, it is inseparable from the character of Oedipus and his past, which is the dramatic engine that drives the action. Unease, foreboding, and despair infuse the atmosphere of the play as this shift becomes deeper and more dangerous to Oedipus.

Portraying conflict is more than a mere listing of external threats. Conflict reveals characters by their response to a threat. A man sent to war is faced with the stark choice: to kill or not to kill. The choice creates anxiety because he fears if he doesn't kill, it means he is a coward who may go to prison and lose the love of those he cares about. If he does kill, he will go against what he believes is human and lose his self-worth. These feelings are rooted in his conscience, what he learned from those closest to him. If he's willing to go to prison rather than kill, that's one kind of character, one that makes belief and spirit primary. If he creates a dodge, a lie to get out of it, that is another kind. One we trust, the other we don't. One is ruled by conscience, the other fear. When a writer creates empathy for the dodging character, the power of the threat is even stronger. In *Hamlet*, Ophelia's response to Hamlet's bizarre behavior comes from the threat that he no longer loves her. Both her father and Hamlet appear to withdraw their love. Yet, if Ophelia found nothing threatening in Hamlet's behavior but instead defied his rejection (and the admonitions of her father), she would become a different character. The consequences would be different. A defiant Ophelia might engage Hamlet's doubt, call out his antics, and become an ally.

The illustration shows the most basic model of conflict. It refers to the scene in which Hamlet comes upon the king, kneeling in prayer (see illus. 1). Looking on, Hamlet says, "Now might I do it pat, now he is a-praying; and now I'll do it" (2.3.73). But he doesn't. Why not? Hamlet cannot act because if he kills the King at prayer, the King will be sent to heaven. Hamlet's father was killed "with all his crimes broad blown." Instead of acting, Hamlet is seized with the fear that to act now will betray his father by helping his murderer to heaven. Can his conscience allow him to kill a man at prayer? Is his inner conflict strong enough to stay his hand, to quench his desire for revenge? It is one of the laces his character creates from the material of his conflict to bind his action. No guards appear, the king is unaware. The opportunity is ripe but conflicted. Conflict overrides his anger and desire for revenge, tying action and conflict together. The illustration shows the choice: do it; don't do it. The conflicted act has the dimensions of thought, doubt, fear—all the elements that are the surface of the conflict that stops the action and chooses, don't do it. Here, then, in conflict is one of the essential levers of action. Conflict regulates action in the way a nozzle regulates the stream of water from a hose.

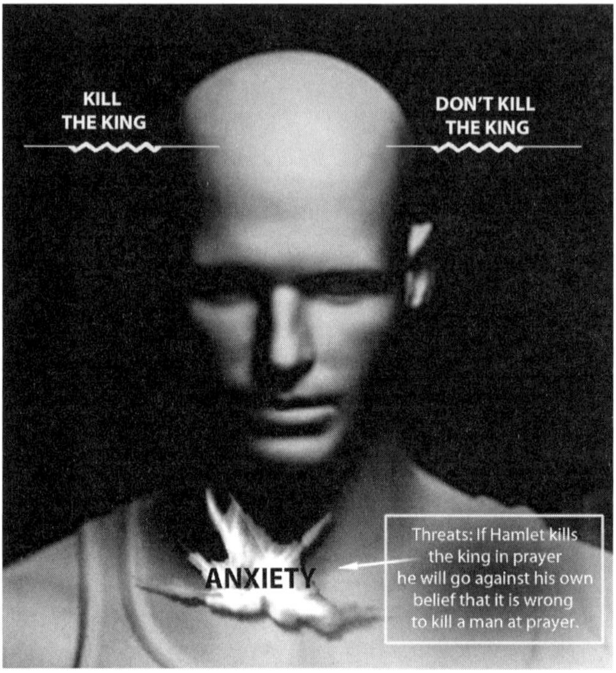

Illustration 1. Basic conflict model. Hamlet discovers the king alone kneeling in prayer.

Practice: King at Prayer Test

The writer can test how well he understands the conflict animating the character with a "king at prayer" test. Can you imagine a situation that powerfully tempts the character to act, but the character doesn't? Write that scene, because whether it ends up in your play or not, you'll learn something you didn't know but will need to know about your character and their world.

Conflict as Story

Writers, above all, are creatures born to tell stories that make sense of what is outside and what is inside. We are all creatures of connection, alive to the joy and suffering that accompany the capacity to love. One of the great paradoxes of humankind is that we lose those we love. We incorporate this reality, in one form or another, into our character as we grow up. Loss of love is one of the deepest threats to our well-being and our sense of place in the world. Love can attach itself to many things besides other persons. The love of God, of country, a cause, an animal may be no less powerful than the love of another person. Unless we are psychopaths, all our actions are enmeshed in our connections, in whom and what we love. The life of every character is created from how the threat of lost love constrains or frees them to act in the world. We turn to stories and particularly drama to show us that we are not alone, that we need not be frozen in our capacity to love and act. Stories show the costs to what we do or don't do and help us hear our greatest fears and our deepest desires for forgiveness and hope. We know how difficult connection and action can be in the world. That difficulty, in the vocabulary of psychology and of drama, is called conflict.

As writers, our primary focus is on characters, the ways they speak, behave, and make connections to each other. That is the raw material we use to tell a story. It is easy to be seduced into seeing characters as people sitting in a café, chatting about trivialities but talk only becomes dramatic when it masks a conflict. The writer seeks to reveal the content and consequence of the conflict through the character's actions. How does she name the laces binding the character and create the scissors that will cut them? If they are not cut, the writer is merely drawing a picture of a status quo. How will a conflict escalate into something volatile and dangerous? What loss is attached to the threat? Is the conflict inside or outside the person or both? Every conflict imposes limits on the character. Drama shows the events that move a character to confront those limits. A conflict can become volatile due to a disconnection among who a character is, what he does, and what he desires.

How does the understanding of threat and conflict enter into the writer's practice? The following are examples that explore different combinations of threat, external and internal, that show how these elements shape action and narrative. In these examples, story is shaped by the way the character exposes threat and conflict.

Take the example of a young man in a small town who is falsely accused of a crime and who runs away. His conflict is whether he should face those who accuse him or flee. He's accused of breaking the law, which threatens his connection to the community, to those closest to him, and to his freedom. He knows he is innocent, but what if people don't believe him? What if he doesn't get a fair trial? He may be black or otherwise different from the rest of the community, or he may just live too close to the edge of trouble. He may be rebellious and respond to the law's external threat by denouncing his accusers and the system. He runs. By not facing his accusers, he has taken the coward's way and risks the loss of self-love. He hitchhikes across the country. He meets someone who teaches him to risk standing and fighting for himself. He learns to survive. The character he meets is likely to see in him a young man with a chip on his shoulder, who chafes at authority, someone who denies the need for connection and acceptance but yearns for them.

Next, take the familiar example of a small western town controlled by a crooked gang led by a corrupt sheriff. They extort money from the town. A stranger comes into town and sees one of the gang humiliating a father in front of his daughter. The stranger disarms and drives off the bully, meets the father with the pretty daughter, and soon sets out to rid the town of the gang. The conflict in this "black hats" versus "white hats" Western is external. The town's citizens are threatened and controlled by the crooks and face threats of violence or loss of livelihood if they resist. We see in the town's refusal to act a conflict that creates an accommodation, a trade of the value of their lives for safety. The stranger's willingness to act needs their help. His appearance is the catalyst that forces the townspeople to choose. Each choice is different, as each person experiences the threat differently. The more intense the threat, the harder the choice. The father with the beautiful daughter is a widower who has no one else except his daughter. How can he risk his daughter? As each person makes a choice and responds to the threat, each creates a different calculation of what makes life worth living.

Another example concerns two young people who meet at a club in New York City. He has a yarmulke pinned on his head. They dance. They talk. She will only tell him her first name. The next week she is there again. They dance again. She agrees to go with him to a café where they eat and talk more. She won't let him take her home. He kisses her. She runs away. He learns where she lives. He goes there the next day and knocks on her door. She opens the door and behind her, hanging on the wall is a Palestinian flag, someone speaks in Arabic from another room. Yes, this looks like *Romeo and Juliet,* two people who should hate each other just because of who they are, but instead they fall in love. If you are a Jew, I can't love you; if you are a Palestinian, I can't love you. The identity of each is dangerous to the other, threatening their connections to those they love and threatening their places in their respective communities. You must be on one side or the other. But this is America, New York. The girl pulls him into her apartment and makes her family meet this surprised young Jewish man. She is fed up with the conflict. She wants to show her family the enemy. Is he? What are their beliefs worth if a simple interaction can't take place that allows both sides to say, "Oh, you are a human being." Her choice is to hate or to love. The threat is that her hate will destroy her ability to love (inside and inside). If she doesn't hate (inside and outside), she can lose those who love her.

Books on dramatic writing all agree on the essential place of conflict in drama. Less time is spent exploring how conflict and character are connected. On the one hand, it seems obvious. A character may desire the throne of England, control of his family, the capture of someone's heart, being loved or successful or the recipient of true justice. Unless a character encounters some resistance, some obstacle to these desires, we will lose interest. We withdraw our emotions from the dramatic events as if they were merely a pageant moving predictably, if colorfully, from one place to another.

Roots of Conflict

The twentieth century gave birth to the way of understanding human action that aligns to the interests and purposes of drama. I am speaking of psychoanalytic theory that reveals conflict through its hidden power over our emotional responses to others. Emotional form is rooted in how we connect to those who are significant in our lives. That connection contains loss and conflict that threads from past to present.

We are creatures defined and animated by conflict. We are also creatures of flesh. Our physicality creates experiences that give meaning to words like grace, vitality, attraction, sensuality, and force. We assess the particular strengths of others. We become adept at reading the personal force of those around us, and we are alert for clues to our own strength in the responses of others to our actions.

Charles Brenner in *The Mind in Conflict* declares that the dynamics of human behavior are inseparable from the dynamics of conflict. Everything we do in conscious life, in daydreams, mistakes, and in dreams expresses the conflicts of our passage from infancy to adulthood. The impression we make on the world, what people describe as our character, is in fact the expression of conflict that has come to define us as individuals, conflict established in what Brenner calls the calamities of childhood that influence our behavior for the rest of our lives (66).

The calamities of childhood are about the losses we experience: loss of a loved one, loss of the love of a loved one, loss of what makes us lovable, and the loss of self-love. The losses of the past play a role in every conflict. The losses become threats to choice and action that are attached to our first conflicts and remain with us. The experience of loss is richly variable. It shapes the content of conflict for a character the writer creates, and it shapes the character's action.

Conflict occurs whenever a desire creates fear or anxiety conscious or unconscious but truly felt (see illus. 2). This is a dynamic that touches every aspect of our mental life. I want that doughnut, that girl, that money, that triumph, that job. I don't want to be fat; she'll think I'm weak; if I have that money, I'll be like the father I hate; if I triumph, I'll defeat my friend and lose his affection; that job is not what I want, but it will keep the respect of my father.

The second illustration expands the model of conflict. When we act, we cannot help but encounter the two realms of our experience: inner life that includes our conscience, and outside reality. The engine of this process is desire—what we want and wish for sets in motion reactions from within and without. Desire is a force like the force of water blasting from a fire hose. Desires in themselves have no inherent morality, no concern for others. They are elemental, instinctual, and aggressive. Desire encounters resistance as others want the same thing and will fight for it. Resistance also may come from within, from conscience or from a threatened loss of love, or fear of rejection, abandonment, hate from another, or self-hatred.

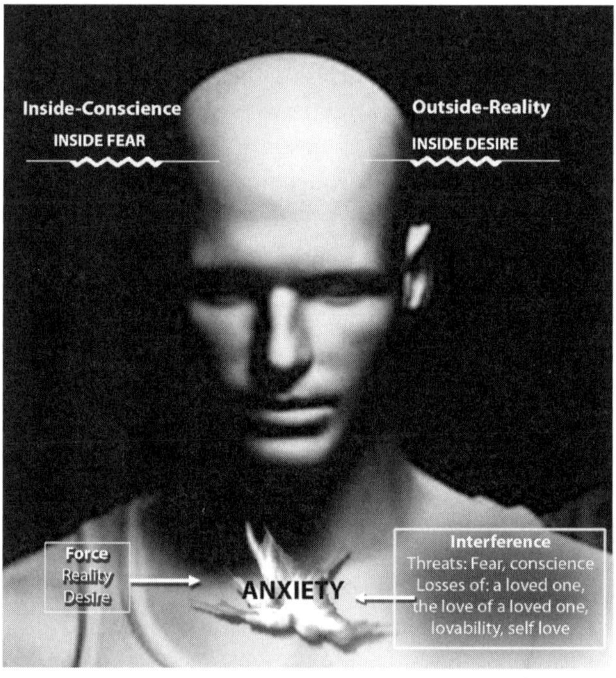

Illustration 2. Expanded conflict model. When constructing conflict, ask between what or whom does it operate? Is it inside or outside? Why does it create anxiety (dramatic tension)?

Emotional form can be seen in the trail of debris left by the struggle between a desire a character can't escape and the resistance that binds that desire. Put another way, a person's conflict is performed, and this performance is indistinguishable from what we call character. We describe this performance through the visible signs conflict makes in our created characters: Hamlet's doubt, his "antic disposition."

How do you reveal a character's desire? Sometimes it can't be spoken aloud or is a secret between characters or is partially revealed. Hally can't say he loves Sam as a father in Fugard's play. It can't be spoken because it threatens the status quo, someone closest to the one who holds the desire will be hurt, and there is a price to be paid. What is the language of a desire that is communicated but not spoken: images, dreams, slips, language that is surprisingly held in check or is unrestrained, wishes, behavior moved by this hidden hand that is understood as the desire is revealed. It isn't the language of explanation. A character's conflict works to distort this subversive desire, submerge it, or build it up like a volcano.

I Am What I Am

Conflict is the very pulse and animate shape of every character. We form these conflicts through experience, through interaction with the ones we love most: father, mother, and sibling. Our emotional life forms a structural pattern of conflicts that define our character through identity with and then separation from our parents, through the development of our conscience, and the development of intense sexual desires. The phases of this development are marked by some difficulty at each stage. Freud compared the development of character to an army passing through a territory that has to leave soldiers behind at different towns to continue the battle in these sites of memory. We carry into every human interaction all of the phases of our development. Think of character as a layered archeological site. Each layer is interrelated and active. Depending on the specific interaction and the threats we face, any one of these layers can penetrate the persona we show publicly. In addition, every significant person in our lives is represented inside our minds. They leave within us an image, some representation of themselves. Thus, we continue to respond to and be affected by the significant people in our lives, even when they are not present. This is no real surprise to dramatists, but it is also, as Brenner writes, a condition that makes analysis possible. The desires that arouse anxiety and defensive behaviors

> constantly find expression in what the patient is thinking and talking about. Depending on the extent to which individual patients are

> able to refrain from editing their thoughts, they will be giving more or less recognizable expression to strivings that arouse unpleasure and defense as they talk. (113–14)

We expect dramatic speech to be as dynamic as the speech of everyday life as it is spoken to the analyst. We expect dialogue to contain the same possibility, to reveal the character's conflict sometimes knowingly and sometimes unknowingly, and often to enhance our view of the conflict by such devices as slips, memories, dreams, and soliloquy and such theatrical elements as poetic speech, song, and movement.

Dialogue is an essential vehicle of dramatic conflict and is never free of emotions that can spin out of the content of the conflict into speech. There is no such thing as dramatic speech that is empty or that doesn't in some way relate to a character's conflict. Nondynamic speech abstracts explain what needs to be shown through action.

In Fugard's play, *"MASTER HAROLD" . . . and the boys*, Hally's speech is a gauge of how close he has come to his conflict over his father. The closer he comes to the reality of his father's presence, the less he can control his speech. He seethes with anger when his mother calls to say she is bringing his father home from the hospital.

> HALLY: He can't hear us from in there. But for God's sake, Mom, what happened? I told you to be firm with him. . . . Then you and the nurses should have held him down, taken his crutches away. . . . I know only too well he's my father! . . . I'm not being disrespectful, but I'm sick and tired of emptying chamber pots full of phlegm and piss. (48)

When he actually speaks to his father, Hally's conflict is in full control suppressing his anger. The fear that he could lose his father is also real.

> HALLY: Welcome home, chum! . . . What's that? . . . Don't be silly, Dad. You being home is just about the best news in the world. . . . (49)

Character dialogue is like the variety of sounds coming from a battle with soldiers spread across a wide plain. In some quarters, all is peaceful, but from others come the sounds of panic and fear. There are celebration and abandon, cries of rage and violence. The volume rises and falls across the plain of conflict, depending on the threats visible on the horizon. We carry inside us representations of all those with whom we've had significant relationships. Each new relationship does not start a new conflict, rather it continues the conflicts that have marked all our relationships.

The fears, needs, risks, and constraints that formed in relation to those we love first we carry forward and involve in every significant relationship.

Brenner speaks of the idea of transference by explaining that every emotionally dynamic relationship with another person "is a new edition of the first, definitive attachments of childhood. Transference is ubiquitous. It develops in every psychoanalytic situation because it develops in every situation where another person is important in one's life" (195). Will every character a writer creates end up being a collection of the conflicts of the character's past? Yes and no. Yes, because that is the source of the structure of character, its dominant conflict. No, because past conflict attaches to our present relationships making a new but familiar misery. Conflict and loss, the past attaching itself to the present, desire pushing toward an objective that is resisted are interesting to the analyst, but to the writer, they are the essential tool kit of emotional form. Like the analyst, the writer searches the emotion within the conflict, but, unlike the analyst, the writer controls the narrative and where it ends. Like the analyst, the writer attempts to penetrate the core dynamic of a character, understanding how conflict forms the nozzle that controls the character's behavioral force. The writer searches for those needs and actions that can open the character to change.

The dynamics of a person's conflict are repeated in all the significant relationships of his or her life. The writer tests emotion and conflict, is drawn to discover whether this repetition will become frozen and end badly or will change from a knowledge gained in experience. The writer's interest in conflict is not only to create the emotional basis for action but also to locate the barriers to change. Change is as significant to emotional form as conflict because change, which may not happen in real life, is the key to the management of endings. A character's conflict sets the limits, that is, the threats that constrain a character that must be breached if a play is to become something more than the eloquent statement of suffering or difficulty, the often spoken of misery of everyday life. Change isn't wining the lottery but experience that creates new knowledge. Hally spits in Sam's face, a painful choosing of fathers, a knowledge that puts at risk the one he loves most.

Find the Cost

Conflict is the essence of mental activity. How do we survive with the pressure conflict creates? We arrange a balance of power among the various threats, a compromise between what we want and what we fear. Our behavior that results from this compromise is what others call our character. The compromise forms the laces binding the desire that plot as emotional form will conspire to cut.

Take a person who may control a trait that arises from the fear created by the opposite, the impulse to merge, to be taken care of. What is so bad about being taken care of? Why should that wish cause fear? What loss can come from gaining this wish? Yet, the person resists giving in to others in every situation. The wish to be cared for can include a forbidden wish, a wish to join with the mother or father. To join with one threatens the loss of the other parent's love. A person with such a conflict can appear as withholding. They withhold their emotion unless the interaction is on their own terms. A writer might describe this character as domineering, aggressive, manipulative, and charming. From the writer's perspective, the character seeks distance due to a fear of giving in, sharing, or being loved. Knowing this is to know the dimensionality of the character, the inner struggle. It allows sympathy for the standoff between the sides of this conflict and allows insight into what the conflict costs the person and those who love him.

A writer can't afford contempt for any character. In one light, our controlling character is a son-of-a-bitch, but to the writer, the character is in emotional danger if that character yields to the desire to give in to another's love. This character combines the need to be unreachable, invulnerable, and the opposite, a yearning to lose control. What can subvert the defense against this character's fear? The writer looks for a situation, a character that recognizes the true desire and allows it into the open to take its chances.

There is, in drama and in life, a dominant conflict within a character that is expressed in all settings, relationships, and struggles. What then is useful in the idea of a protagonist and antagonist? For the character, the world, however represented, is the stage of that character's conflict. The world doesn't define the character who walks on its stage. It places obstacles in the way of the character, testing him with threats that engage his deepest fears. The antagonist does not create the conflict. The antagonist is like a hammer driving a wedge into the main character, forcing the content of the conflict into the open, and showing the costs of keeping it hidden. Without pressure from an antagonist in whatever form, the main character will simply continue on desperately grasping the status quo.

Hosed

The story of a character is the story of that character's dominant conflict. The dominant traits of character, or personality, are visible in the character's manner, speech, range of feeling, dress, movement, capacity for connection, and power to act. In the notion of character as fire hose, a character's conflict acts like the nozzle controlling the intensity, spread, and strength of the stream of action made visible by words, thoughts, choices, feelings, and physical behavior. In addition to the base line of force, we are aware of where the hose is pointing and whether it can be adjusted to fit the circumstances: a light spray for the flowers or a blast at the wild dog that wanders into the yard.

We experience character as a force that comes toward us. We constantly adjust to that force before going into head-on encounter, by bobbing and weaving, or charming and seducing. When an in-your-face-guy meets a bob-and-weave-guy, we watch the struggle of one who blows hot, who pushes language down below the neck with cursing, sexuality, and insult, while the other blows cold and pushes language up above the neck, trying to stay in control through reason and rules.

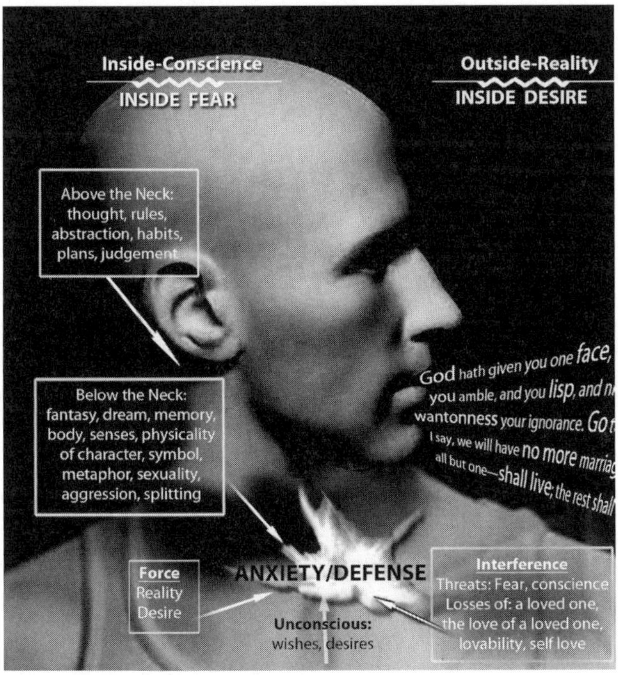

Illustration 3. Full conflict model. Dramatic dialogue moves above and below the neck.

Illustration 3, representing a developed model of conflict that shows a picture of the dynamics of internal conflict, employs a dynamic geography. A character's needs and wishes may be ready to push up from below the neck in the traditional shorthand for the intercutting between conscious and unconscious mind. Always present below the surface of our rule-bound mind, holding to our conscience and protective routines, is the restive and insistent domain of desire. Our body, our appetites, our dreams, fantasy and memory, our aggression—our needs aroused unbidden—all these live and strain against the realm above that pretends to be in charge.

Our defenses construct barriers of right and wrong to compromise with the pressure below the neck. Our language is the outward sign of this inner, often unconscious, turmoil. Words and the impulses behind them stray back and forth across the dividing line, sending out flares of emotion in this battle. Our unconscious also takes the stage in our fantasies and dreams, our bodies and sexuality, only to contend with the rational, orderly, moral forces above the neck: our conscience. The writer, however, is free to cross the line between above and below and, like the child, make characters talk to imaginary people, bring back the dead, receive visits from angels, split a character into two parts and hold a conversation between them, introduce mysterious strangers who bear messages, make animals talk, and do any other things that invention may propose.

This model means to point to the complexity inherent in speech and behavior, a map of the forces that are in dramatic play to create the illusion of life.

Let's return to Hamlet to illustrate the full model. After Hamlet's encounter with the ghost of his father, he is not led to immediate action despite learning his father was murdered by the usurping king. Hamlet is held in check by his doubts. Was the spirit his father or some demon from hell working to destroy him? To stalk this doubt, he tells Horatio not to remark on or admit to any knowledge of his behavior as he assumes an "antic disposition." Hamlet's strategy of assuming "madness" is a stratagem of concealment, an improvisation in which the language "below the neck" seemingly untethers from reason. The first time we see Hamlet improvise his disposition is with Polonius. Hamlet starts his improvisation by answering Polonius's question, "Do you know me, my lord?" with "Excellent well. You are a fishmonger." Hamlet then plays this as a riff on honesty, age, and the ripeness of his daughter. But these are word games played on an old man for whom he has affection. Something entirely different happens when Hamlet encounters Ophelia and again tries to improvise his "disposition." The exchange with Ophelia is an example of the workings of the full conflict model. The scene is framed by what we know has preceded: both Laertes and Polonius have warned Ophelia away from Hamlet on the grounds that, as a prince, he is not to be trusted. He will use his position to dazzle and then take advantage of her. Her father has instructed Ophelia to refuse him admittance to her company, which she does. Before this meeting, Ophelia tells her father that Hamlet appeared to her his clothes in disarray, looked piteously on her, touched her, sighed, and held her in his gaze as he left but said nothing. On the basis of this report, Polonius has arranged this "chance" meeting with Hamlet that she knows is observed by the king and her father. Here we learn whether Hamlet can contain his acted improvisation of the language below the neck, the stuff of conflicted desire, dream, fear, and anger, using the same clever word play he practiced on her father. Or, will it erupt into something that will reveal the contending forces in his character?

Ophelia's first gesture, after the briefest of greetings, is to ask Hamlet to take back his letters and writings. His immediate answer is to deny he gave them to her. She responds by handing them directly to him: "Rich gifts wax poor when givers prove unkind." Both immediately are in "it." Anyone can recognize a lover's quarrel as it bursts like a squall. Hamlet, stung by her insistent rejection, laughs in disbelief, "Are you honest?" Then when she doesn't understand, he joins his words to a deeper feeling.

OPHELIA: My Lord?
HAMLET: Are you fair?
OPHELIA: What means, your lordship?
HAMLET: That if you be honest and fair, your honesty should admit no discourse to your beauty.

Hamlet barely covers his accusation that she is being dishonest; her gesture to return his letters is false to her real feelings. She remains steadfast.

OPHELIA: Could beauty, my lord, have better commerce than with honesty?
HAMLET: Ay, truly; for the power of beauty will sooner transform honesty from what it is to a bawd than the force of honesty can translate beauty into his likeness. This was sometime a paradox, but now the time gives it proof. I did love you once. (1.1.105–15)

What has happened? After Ophelia faced his accusation that she is not speaking her true feelings, Hamlet's language changes. Ophelia is caught in her conflicted feelings as both lover and daughter. She knows her father is listening and so cannot disobey his demand that she rebuff Hamlet. Confronted by Ophelia's unwillingness to state her feelings, Hamlet suddenly finds his mind goaded into a conflict deeper than a lover's spat over letters. Ophelia's resistance loosens her identity as Ophelia and joins her to the identity of the woman false to her feelings, one whose honesty is like a bawd. In Hamlet's life, the analogous woman is the one who so quickly abandoned his loving father for the bed of his uncle. Hamlet's language now becomes unhinged from Ophelia and attached to this deeper conflict and the emotions it releases. As if to warn Ophelia that all is changed in his mind to something he cannot reconcile, he tells her, "I did love you once."

Ophelia tries to pull him back, "Indeed, my lord, you made me believe so." Hamlet, his anger rising, tells her she should not believe him; virtue cannot stick to our sinning nature. "I loved you not." With "Get thee to a nunnery," Hamlet lets loose a tirade fueled by yearning, shame, and anger. We don't believe for a minute that this is the clever posing of an "antic disposition." This is Hamlet's conflict about Gertrude as yielding consort to his father's murderer; it breaks through the control of reason and judgment and overtakes his language. This new language comes from below the neck attached to his fear and threatens his place in the love of both his mother and father. We become aware that Hamlet is addressing his mother as his attack turns to the deceitful sexual nature of women.

> HAMLET: I have heard of your paintings too, well enough: God hath given you one face, and you make yourselves another. You jig, you amble, and you lisp, and nickname God's creatures, and make your wantonness your ignorance. Go to, I'll no more on't; it hath made me mad. I say, we will have no more marriages. Those that are married already, all but one, shall live; the rest shall keep as they are. To a nunnery go. (3.1.139–45)

To Ophelia's, "O, What a noble mind is here o'erthrown!" we can add, "That is the writer's job." Hamlet is caught in his own stratagem of improvising a character loosely tied to reason and fair judgment when the very language he meant to use to convey the feint overwhelms him with the real force of conflicted emotion.

Practice: Finding Trouble

The writer grows and nurtures the terrain of a play's beginning, the world in which the character comes into focus. How deep is a character's trouble? There are present and past elements to that trouble. If we are correct that conflict and threat are bound up in the writer's own character, then the writer should be able to access this dynamic. There is an automatic writing exercise familiar to teachers of writing that helps the writer evade the control of the forces above the neck. Prepare to write for five minutes. Once you put pen to paper, you cannot stop writing until five minutes have passed. Don't pause to think. Keep writing, no matter what comes out. Write as the character in the play you are working on. Write a speech by that character. Don't try to predetermine what the character will say. What you write may not be from any character or voice you immediately recognize. The point of the exercise is to remove the control of judgment from your writing.

You can't hold content outside like a fancy shirt that you'll put on when you want to show off. The words that launch your play, not essay, not letter to my public, not random thoughts in dialogue, but a play, come from the body, at first your body but then the actor's. You give a name to the body that speaks these words. The named body lives in time, in place, in the detail of physical and emotional life. Just like yours.

Example. *The chair I'm sitting in is yellow with crappy brown spots. I know who is knocking at the door. I don't want to see them. Go away. If I don't open the door, I'm going to turn into a stone. If I do, I'll go blind. I kept this chair when we broke up. I count the crappy brown spots. They glow in the dark. People have chairs like this all over the city. We recognize each other. It has nothing to do with money or success. We have the same chair. I can tell by their eyes, their shoes. I pissed in the wastebasket last night. I wanted to pretend it was my lawn and the moon was full. I could feel the wind. I could see the trees. Voices asked where I was. I didn't tell them.*

Conflict has content. Speak it. Let the conflict find its voice as it animates the name and body you've given it. It's always on about being messed with on that day. It wasn't right, it was wrong your brother called. He's coming over. Always on about his frigging success. What about me? Look at me. You look sick. He's always on about money, like it was alive. It can hear us. Why don't we have any? Ask it. Always on about how smart he is. People are weak. Take what you want. That girl at the bank? Have her clothes off by the end of the week. Bet. The dynamics of conflict are abstract forms that are filled with the content of words, feelings, thoughts that bring the past into the present. They freeze the present with repetition, give reality to what is pressing for change, give expression to the danger of losing forward progress, give feeling sound, and give meaning language.

Making Change: Margulies' *Loman Family Picnic*

The Loman Family Picnic by Donald Margulies masterfully mixes the contending languages above and below the neck in a theatricalized mix of comedy and drama. We can look at this play for how conflict binds the characters and how emotional form traces the scissoring of these restraints and the consequence. If we follow Doris and Herbie's route, can we see it create the credible conditions of change at the end? The constraints on expression put their relationship at risk. Richly conflicted, they live in a story that uses a ghost, literary appropriation, a child's imagination, and a faux multiple-choice ending. These devices are not just tricks of the trade, a nod to much-used comic turns to keep the audience awake, they are an essential part of the play's emotional form.

Doris, the main character, simultaneously states and denies her conflict in both language and behavior. A desire to flee her life pulls at her speech like an undertow. Her life with husband, Herbie, holds her in check through kids, habit, humor, fantasy, and fear. Fighting against the undertow is her fear of losing life itself, the fear of losing her connection to normalcy, her fear of shame, her fear her mother will refuse her. Caught as she is, should she be counted among the living or the dead? We witness the struggle as her speech moves back and forth across the line dividing feelings above and below the neck. This is how Margulies begins his play.

Doris, thirty-eight years old, wearing a housecoat over her pajamas, sits on the sofa with her wedding dress on her lap. She is cutting it to shreds with a pair of scissors.

DORIS (*To us.*): . . . Last night was my wedding anniversary. Eighteen years. Herbie had to work, what else is new. I love the way my life has turned out. Did I say that already? On the day I was married the world showed every sign of coming to an end . . .

Mitchell, eleven years old, enters through the front door carrying schoolbooks.

DORIS: What are you doing home from school?
MITCHELL: School let out; the day is over; I came home. It's three-thirty.
DORIS: Oh, my God. You're home from school and I haven't been out all day? I didn't even put on any clothes? I'm not depressed.
MITCHELL: I didn't say you were depressed. What are you doing with your wedding gown?

DORIS: I got the greatest idea for a Halloween costume—you're gonna love this: the Bride of Frankenstein.
MITCHELL: You're gonna tear up your wedding gown for a costume?
DORIS: I'm not disenchanted with my marriage.
MITCHELL: I didn't say you were disenchanted with your marriage.
DORIS: I still love your father.
MITCHELL: I didn't say you didn't.
DORIS: I love my life. I love the way my life has turned out. Your father doesn't bore me. What if your father and I got a divorce? Who would you live with? Never mind, only kidding. So, how was school today?
MITCHELL: I owe Miss Schoenberg fifty cents for lunch. You forgot to put lunch in my lunchbox again.
DORIS: Did I? Oh, honey, I'm sorry. I'm not a negligent mother.
MITCHELL: I didn't say you were. I said you forgot. Anyone could forget.
DORIS: I guess I was just preoccupied with how much I love my life. Don't you love this room? Isn't it unusual? I need a job. I have to get out of the house. (199–201)

This is both comic and horrible. To use the "hose" metaphor, her character is unable to control when and where it sprays. What does the son of such a mother do? He defends against the fear of loss coming off his mother like smoke from a fire as he says, "So I'm writing this musical-comedy version of *Death of a Salesman* called *Willy*!" (213–14).

How difficult is it to imagine something that will change the struggle embedded in the conflict? What can change Doris's feelings about her life? If only Herbie would come home with flowers, or dance her around the living room and sing to her, or just pay attention to his family. Would that do it? Would that make her stop talking to her dead sister? If it is a true dramatic conflict, Herbie's actions can't do that. If the play is about the moment when they did figure it out, we would call it a soap opera.

Dramatic conflict isn't fixed by cosmetic changes. Creating emotional form from the dynamics of conflict does not imagine human character as a car engine that needs adjustment. Creating emotional form means that Doris is conflicted about love itself, not just about Herbie. The wreck of their relationship is as much about her—who she is and what she is capable of doing and feeling—as it is about Herbie. She has put herself in a vise by her choices, a vise that keeps her safe from the risks her sister took that ended in suicide. The vise she chose was Herbie. The play's emotional form reveals the power of this vise.

Their struggle is heading toward a breaking point. We don't know how yet, but we know it is tied to the man who stood next to her on the day she wore her wedding dress—the one she is ripping up at the opening.

The writer creates an individuality of voice for each character caught in conflict. The depth of the conflict shapes the individuality of voice, its inherent humor, hallucination, sadness, and rage. Individuality of voice isn't found in the ratiocinations of characters who comment on issues, or mere contests of wit, or explanations that freeze the dynamics of content. It is found in the unique, uncontrollable mix of language and feeling that blossoms from the past and present of a character in conflict.

When Herbie enters, it is night. Doris and his two sons, Mitch and Stewie, are asleep on the couch in front of the TV. He sets down a bag of groceries and unloads both himself and the shopping bag.

HERBIE: Daddy's home! The provider is here! (*He waits, expecting to be greeted ceremoniously, but his sleeping family doesn't budge. Facetiously.*) Gee, it's good to be back in my family's waiting arms! In the bosom of my family! Don't all of you jump up and kiss me at once! (*A beat.*) Daddy's home! Another day, another dollar! The warrior is back! I'm black and blue but I'm back in one piece! From a whole day of busting my balls for you! Gee, I can't wait to get up at six A.M. so they can be pounded to bits all over again! Oh!, but look what Daddy brought! Wow! What a guy! What a dad! (*Unloads as he speaks.*) (206–7)

Doris wakes and feeds him dinner, a dietetic tuna salad, as if to say here, eat, be thinner because, as you are, you are not what I want. The play breaks from reality at this moment as Herbie and Doris have their warmest scene in the play. But the scene is just a fantasy they create. In the scene, they each warmly describe the moment the other dies—Doris from a heart attack and Herbie from multiple organ failures. We marvel at the lively warmth as they recount each other's deaths. The scene theatricalizes the aggression each feels for the other's death wrapped in the emotional intimacy of a dinner conversation. The fantasy makes clear that flowers and song will not solve the play's central conflict, their painful lives.

Unlike Doris, Herbie's conflict doesn't lead him to statements such as, "I love the way my life has turned out." He can remember poverty, six kids in three rooms. He can't remember when his kids were born or even the date of his own birth. He doesn't remember his father touching him, even shaking his hand. He went through most of his life as he goes through his day, "eyes shut tight and holding my breath," waiting to come home, but what's there (222)? He says he is afraid to speak for fear of saying the wrong thing, of being shot down.

HERBIE (*To us.*): So I shut up a long time ago. It was a decision I made after something happened, something I don't remember what. I remember deciding well, fuck-'em-all one day, and Doris has handled it ever since. I let her do the talking. What the hell, I save my breath. (223)

Still, Herbie is astonished when Doris bursts into the room in her ripped-up wedding dress as the Bride of Frankenstein. She is excited to take the boys trick or treating for Halloween. Doris's torn wedding dress is the provocation she surely knew it would be. She claims it was not something meant to hurt. Who believes this?

HERBIE: The dress you wore to your wedding. It's supposed to mean so much. How does a girl rip up—

DORIS: I was never gonna wear it again. It was getting old and faded hanging at the back of my closet eighteen years; what's the matter with you? All of a sudden you're gonna take it personal? "The Bride of Frankenstein." (*As she goes to kitchen.*) God, Herbie, where's your sense of humor? (228–29)

Doris won't accept what she fully intended to do. In full denial, she asks the unexpressive Herbie to sing "Autumn Leaves." She's happy. The dress still fits her. She wants him to enter her fantasy. Can he be someone he isn't? She wants him to sing to her, pay no attention to the wrecked dress.

The nozzle of Doris's conflict is restricted by innocence and aggression. Her words fly out, striking many targets at once. Herbie's nozzle is restricted by fear and need. Herbie fears speech, just like Doris fears love. Calling these two protagonist and antagonist is only one part of their reality. The more significant part for writer and audience is how profoundly they are in conflict with themselves. She chose him to deny herself love, while he believes he doesn't deserve love and so has no way to ask for it.

Emotional form doesn't imagine change as mechanical, but it does imagine dynamic and eruptive events that create transformation. The conflicted world of a character can change if the resistance to recognizing their deepest feeling is confronted by a new experience or knowledge that alters what has been held fixed. The dysfunctional drama of this family carries the play only so far, then it will stall and turn repetitive unless something shatters the status quo. That something is Stewie's impending bar mitzvah, which uncovers the content clamped down in Herbie's conflict both as promise and threat. Will it lead Herbie and Doris to an experience of themselves and their conflict that can change their lives?

The event comes after the bar mitzvah celebration at home, after mom tries to dance with her "men," when Stewie is counting the money from his gifts. Herbie, in a twisted mix of sentiment and cruelty, takes Stewie's gift money away because he needs the money to pay for the bar mitzvah.

A fight erupts. Mitchell tries to get between them and is shoved away. Stewie hits his father, "HE HATES US, MOMMY! HE HATES US!" Doris holds the boys, and Herbie screams, "YOU THINK I DON'T LOVE YOU?!! YOU THINK I DON'T LOVE YOU?!!" (250). What does he have in this house? Herbie has nothing. He has his ratty underwear. He has the junk in his bureau drawer. He rips out the drawer to show them.

> WHAT DO I HAVE! I HAVE NOTHING! I HAVE SHIT! I HAVE THE TOILET FOR TEN MINUTES IN THE MORNING! I DON'T EVEN HAVE YOU! . . . THIS IS ME?!! THIS IS MY LIFE! THIS DRAWER IS MY WHOLE LIFE, RIGHT HERE, THIS DRAWER! (251–52)

He throws it on the floor and storms out.

Name That Ending

The event of the bar mitzvah is a way for the writer to show his hand, the core of emotional form. What will Herbie and Doris do with this experience? Margulies asks us to play Name That Ending and presents four alternates. In the first, Doris tells him the marriage is over.

> I can't run your public relations anymore, Herbie. Eighteen years; that's not so bad. Nothing to be ashamed of. Who says you have to be married to just one person your whole life? (261)

In the second, Doris jumps off her balcony. She tells Herbie,

> My life is over, Herbie. I have the boys, but I don't have them; they won't be mine much longer. They'll survive; children do. Children never remember the good stuff anyway, they only remember the shit. (262)

In the third, Doris tells Herbie how much she needs him, that she never felt so lonely as when he ran out. Herbie's response is to sing her a verse of "Autumn Leaves" as the two boys run to embrace their parents.

In the last ending, nothing appears to change. Doris gets angry that he ate bon bons at the movies. She gets his tuna plate and tells him to sit. She sits beside him as he eats. Mitchell watches them as they say the last lines of the play.

HERBIE: (*Sheepishly.*) Doris, look, I'm sorry about—
DORIS: Don't. (*A beat. Quietly.*) Don't. (264)

Which of these four endings completes the emotional form of the play? We know the real ending. We treat the others as dramatic fantasies that the characters, as we know them, cannot perform. We briefly view the characters through the lenses of different endings so that we feel the falseness of each ending, until we come to the true one.

Margulies' approach creates the emotional jolt of recognition that Doris and Herbie cannot break free from the conditions of their relationship. The real ending is more than a cold slice of reality that settles into focus as the last of his multiple endings. Herbie and Doris up to this point have shown that the compromises we create to tame the power of conflict are a prison, a testament to our fears that make us helpless in the face of our needs for love and connection. Can new knowledge and experience alter the foundations of those fears?

Margulies answers this with Mitch's musical of the family picnic. The musical scene is prologue to the end of the play. Mitch's musical dramatizes our hope that things will work out. He gives voice to the fact that we have the same wish that Mitchell does. The musical gives us both the pleasure of entertainment and the pleasure of seeing the characters defy their emotional blinders. In the glow of the music and Mitch's fantasy, we hear Doris say,

DORIS: He's not a dreamboat,
No Casanova.
But he will be my man
Until my life is over.
Am I right? Am I wrong?
Am I blind?
He's mine!
Don't mock him, Mitchell!
Don't snicker, Stewie
For though you may believe
He's dull, or dumb, or screwy,
When he walks through that door,
It's a sign—
He's mine!
. . . .
I know your soles are hurting,
I know your soul can sing. (255–58)

Coming on the heels of Herbie's blowup and exit, the musical scene abruptly dissipates and reconstitutes the feelings of fear and rage into their precise opposite. We know Mitchell's scene is a fantasy, yet we can't deny that hearing Doris say the words has an impact.

During Herbie's blowup, Doris is barely able to speak, quietly trying to calm him. Her reaction to his exit is to cry out his name. Doris for the first time recognizes the pain that Herbie feels and never expressed. Mitch's musical takes flight on the hope of this recognition. Mitch's fantasy of the family picnic boldly conjures a family happy with each other. The reality is that his family lacks the ability to speak with acceptance and recognition of their pain.

The event of the bar mitzvah overwhelmed the characters, creating a recognition in Doris. What does this recognition lead to? Margulies eliminates the melodramatic possibilities with his optional endings: divorce, suicide, and sudden reconciliation. The true ending expresses the depth of his respect and love for his characters. Yes, Doris is the Jewish mother fussing over what Herbie eats, but she has made him the tuna salad, and she sits down with him. When he tries to apologize, the resolution is found in her answer. Doris first says, "Don't." This may mean that what has changed between them has only changed for the worse; they will live in a colder hell than before. She is ready to take his head off. But, no, there is a beat. She quietly says, "Don't," a second time. She has chosen to stay connected. She is not a different person, nor is he. She can act on her understanding of his pain and show him acceptance, if not forgiveness. He can speak his pain and know hers, all signs of love.

Bearings: Talk Worth the Trouble

Writers work with the medium of speech. But speech is a kind of behavior that people use to deny and obscure as much as to connect or to assault. It is a three-dimensional chess of the heart. We know we are not trustworthy, that we are afraid, that we fiercely desire, with no care for the consequences. So when we sit alone in the audience waiting for the curtain to rise, we are conflicted between the fear that the artist will show us that complexity and the hope we will be let off the hook.

We love speech. It is the way we test our presence. It is like Ariadne's thread that we use to find our way out of the labyrinth in which we contend with what is hidden and feared. We love speech because it is one of the purest signs of the spirit at play. Children know this and mark their worlds with invented language. We love speech because it is our litmus test for the truth of intimacy. We are also wary. It reveals, it hurts, it incites, it can light a match to resentment or jealousy.

The playwright is not just a clever stiff putting words into mouths; the writer for the stage is shaping the lives that animate those words. Conflict that binds desire also shapes that life. A character's clever and confident advice can be a recipe for catastrophe. We love to watch aghast as the incident unwinds, Doris and her wedding dress. A character heartbreakingly expresses faith in someone who can't be true, Nora in her doll's house. We watch to see what it will cost and how it will be known. Characters are locked in a devilish geography of words that bind them to a past, to an injury, to a secret, and we, the audience, wait always for speech to fail.

Although the audience may wait, the writer knows exactly where that failure will happen. It is one of the stations on the writer's journey to the end. Snipping the laces that bind desire requires a knowledge of conflict and the craft of making an ending. The desire is emotionally credible because it is conflicted and crafted by an insight into the workings of conflict. It is not an unmoored desire to do just anything or just go crazy.

Dionysus teaches us that we live with an inner life and we resist its forces as they surge and ignite us at our peril. Psychology tells us that who we are is defined by how we are in all those past conflicts with those closest to us. Emotional form is the articulation of what happens when the hoops that bind character are loosened. The plotting of emotional form is knowing where and when to cut the binding cords. If the writer, flush with skill, simply makes a disturbance for the sake of the noise and the excitement, then he is playing at drama, not writing drama. He gives us the outer show but not the cost and meaning of the disturbance. Margulies disturbs the world of Doris and Herbie. He gives a lesson in the theatrical tools a writer can use to expose conflict. He does not magically release his characters from their conflicts. He holds to the discipline of emotional form by reconstituting the status quo that has been utterly changed through the pain of hidden feeling.

One way we describe attention is to say you hang on someone's words. Hanging as in, if we let go, we will fall from that place without seeing and knowing what is being revealed. An audience during the course of a play sometimes is said to hang on every word. Lucky is the writer who can achieve this, but a writer can't do it without the knowledge of endings. Audiences don't want to know what to expect, but they want the writer to know. Hanging on every word suggests a submission to the ending, a readiness to see the best endangered by the worst and a trust that it will bring meaning. The writer's gift of speech is challenged by the inevitability of an ending and the shaping force of emotion. Why are endings so hard, and what can we say about them?

3. The End Is Where You Started

> TYRONE: Mary! For God's sake, forget the past!
> MARY: (*With strange objective calm.*) Why? How can I? The past is the present, isn't it? It's the future, too. We all try to lie out of that but life won't let us.
>
> —Eugene O'Neill, *Long Day's Journey into Night*

Is it possible to exaggerate the importance of endings? Endings exist only in the light shone by a beginning and a middle. The writer knows he has to stop at some point and write, "The End." Endings come in many ways: life ends for others and for us; relationships end between friends and lovers. The-all-too-short moments of our lives end: childhood, youth, and middle age. Stories have ends that we've anticipated since first hearing, knowing them more fully once we become the storytellers. The notorious problems of act 2 come largely from the difficulty of ending a play. The ending is the specter that looms from the moment the writer sketches the opening. Emotional form is the art of the ending.

There are two major kinds of endings: (1) those that transform all that has gone before, where embedded in the end is a recognition of the beginning and the middle, which builds the need for closure and new meaning; and (2) those that resist closure as false interruptions and substitute a continuity that doesn't transform but intensifies, as in the endings of *Waiting for Godot* or Sarah Kane's *Blasted.*

Good endings are inescapable; they are both thrilling and oppressive. In his book on the structure of narrative, *Reading for the Plot,* critic Peter Brooks asks what the difference is between living and narrating. When you narrate, you appear to start with a beginning. He turns for an answer to Jean-Paul Sartre and his protagonist Roquentin in *La Nausée.*

> You say, It was a fine autumn evening in 1922. I was a notary's clerk in Marommes. But, says Roquentin: In reality you have started at the end. It is there, invisible and present, it is what gives these few words the pomp and value of a beginning. "I was out walking, I had left the town without realizing it, I was thinking about my money troubles." This sentence, taken simply for what it is, means that the guy was absorbed, morose, a hundred miles from an adventure, exactly in a mood to let things happen without noticing them. But the end is there, transforming, everything. (92–93)

Endings can make the writer crazy, think that some choice is just out of sight that would make all the difference. Endings make the writer feel stupid, as in "This is a test, and I'm flunking." Endings create a resistance because the end implies a death: the stopping of time, the showing of cards, the consequence made visible.

An Exception to the Rule?

Emotional form is conceived in the classical world and the birth of drama. A dramatic narrative creates a pattern of action driven by the deepest emotional forces within the writer and, thus, the character. A character may not know, or understand, these forces out of an ignorance of self and what is most meaningful in life. These hidden and conflicted forces become the catalyst for emotional meaning. Being hidden to the character doesn't mean the forces in conflict are passive, just the opposite. From the beginning of a play, they, like the bull kicking at the fence gate, move the action forward until it breaks loose, wreaking havoc and forcing change. If this pattern makes one kind of rule, there are always exceptions.

June Schlueter addresses this from the view of modern criticism in *Dramatic Closure: Reading the End.*

> And, like tragedy and comedy, which consistently found definition in their treatment of the end, the plays of writers variously classified as "modern," "postmodern," "avant-garde," or "absurd" may be said to mark a modern genre, persistent in its testing and contesting of the end.

Contesting the end comes with the ideology of an era or movement.

> Insistently interrogative, modern drama explicitly revisions the tacit contract between play and reader that offers the drama as an explanatory system and as a conventionally aesthetic organic whole. (60)

You can certainly write plays that resist emotional form or plays defined by a character who does not change, whose resistance is integral to the universe of the play. *Waiting for Godot* is an example. Less-famous, student playwrights often put forward points of view or states of being. Plays can be driven more by thought than narrative action, more by rhetoric or poetic expression. These plays do not find their reason for being in the transforming power of emotional experience but in the power of language and idea. These plays create rhetorical and experimental techniques of resisting that very power, or in some cases, they reach it by other means. Contemporary Americans who write such plays include Mac Wellman,

Suzan-Lori Parks, Erik Ehn, and Eric Overmyer. They didn't completely make this up. Their works are connected to the major forces of the avant-garde at the beginning of the twentieth century. Expressionism became a wrecking crew of the well-made play and constraints on language and plot. Frank Wedekind, Georg Kaiser, and the early Brecht allied with the experiments of the dadaists, the surrealists, Antonin Artaud, and the theater of the absurd.

Is who we are always in the mix of endings? Endings may cause a variety of strategies, but the writer as a person cannot be separated from the ending. The writer has beliefs, views about politics, hope, love, and nature. He has strong feelings about things over which he has little control. An ending isn't separate from who we are but is entangled in our seminal desires, and our beliefs about human nature, and about truth. An ending is to emotional form as purpose is to action. Unmoored from the content of the ending, emotional form is like real life, a continuity whose shape is hidden. Emotional form carries in the conflicted matter of its content the possible outcomes of change or blindness to change that will shape the end.

The classic concept of the end is that it is a vortex that draws everything in the play to it. The simplest statements or actions at the beginning have in them the certain knowledge of the end. We use ends as the lens to gain true sight of any number of things, such as, wars, love affairs, political deals, even life itself. The end changes what seemed random or confusing and imbues it with a purpose, a meaning. If we didn't need meaning, would we ever concern ourselves with endings? Just stop when you can't think of anything else to say. What does it matter? Endings make clear that nothing will ever be the same again. If the story doesn't reach that nexus of transformation, we are still in the middle, a place of repetition, of search for meaning, an endless self-therapy. A play without an end is what emotional form is in real life, hidden but never brought to light as only a drama can.

The Riddle of the Middle

What is the functional relationship between middles and ends? If the ending is the organizing principle of emotional form, the core desire, how does it flow from beginning, to middle, to end? Often, writers feel they are groping their way blindly toward an end. Or perhaps they have an ending and grope toward a beginning. They are like the patient in therapy, the analysand, working with the analyst to gain insight into the present so they can change how they understand the past.

Psychoanalysis is a model of working from an unknown end, the meaning of our behavior, back through a middle and a beginning. This process is analogous to a writer following a path through emotional form toward an end that is not simply an intellectual construct imposed on events but rather an emergent, new understanding culled from emotional experience. Brooks in a series of lectures published as *Psychoanalysis and Storytelling* describes the connection of this process to transference.

> [T]he notion of "transference"—is of course itself a representation, perhaps an allegory, of interaction or transaction. In the transference, the analysand constitutes himself as a subject by way of the dialogic and dialectic presence of the analyst, in a dynamic or erotic interaction. Furthermore, the whole relationship is metaphoric, in that it is based on the analyst's role as surrogate for past figures of authority, and the revival of infantile scenarios of satisfaction that are reproduced and replayed as if they were of the present. Freud repeatedly describes the transference as a realm of the "as-if" as an "artificial illness," and as a "new edition or reprint" of an old text. (42)

Therapy begins with the patient's need to address behaviors and feelings that are disrupting the patient's life and makes that life miserable. The patient wants to retell the story of a past but casts the analyst in the story, as if the analyst were a significant figure from the patient's past. The patient then begins to repeat the psychic dynamic of the past with the analyst. These repetitions are marked by comments and interpretations by the analyst. As Brooks says, "The analyst . . . must deal with the actuality of a force—the force of past desire unconsciously enacting itself in the present—while ever attempting to translate it back into the terms of the past, in which it can recover its meaning" (*Reading for the Plot*, 227).

The end of this process, if successful, is the discovery of new meaning that can modify destructive loops of repetition and allow the patient's psychic life to move forward. At the end of this process, the past is still the past, but the new meaning gained provides a critical difference to the patient: "In other words, the transference, like the text as read, becomes the peculiar space of a deadly serious play, in which affect, repeated from the past, is acted out as if it were present, yet eventually in the knowledge that the persons and relations involved are surrogates and mummers" (*Reading for the Plot*, 234).

This "deadly serious play" is the process of emotional form, in which a writer works with the conflicted emotional material inscribed in characters and events, who create narratives real or fantastic, who strive for meaning through endings, and who serve as the mummers of the writer's inner world. The terms and outcome of this "play" are unique to the writer. The writer struggles to clarify the emotional meaning that is gathering in the play. This involves three strenuous efforts: (1) seeking the links of present to past, (2) yielding to the needs of the characters, and (3) crossing the boundaries of resistance to find the truth of the characters voice and the consequences of their action.

For the writer, getting past the middle is like the task of the analyst who understands the dynamic affecting the patient's behavior but who knows it does no good to reveal it at the beginning. Time is required for the patient to interpret and then integrate a new meaning. Writers experience the end's relation to the middle in much the same way. Brooks quotes from Roland Barthes, who argues that without the middle—a space of retard, postponement, error, and partial revelation—there is no meaning that can be created by the end (*Reading for the Plot*, 92). The middle establishes credibility for what is to come. Events must take time. The old saw "Show, don't tell" is a nod to the need for time. "Telling" short-circuits lived experience for the character and the audience. Showing is the most basic way to win credibility. It is embedded in the distinction between "talking the talk and walking the walk." Brooks writes, "The desire of the text is ultimately the desire for the end, for that recognition which is the moment of the death of the reader in the text" (*Reading for the Plot*, 108). It is late, and you're lost, deep in the dark middle of the play. The danger of the middle is that we love to talk and we think we're good at it. We're enthralled and aroused by the sound of voices in our head, coming from our character, and we don't want to stop. The end is a matter of discipline as much as it is of structure and insight.

Practice: Ask the Character

To find the recognition that marks the end, we push deep enough to know the blindness and destructiveness in the central character. Push to know the fear of taking action, the fear that came from the threat of greater pain or loss. The middle is about the emotional barrier to moving ahead. To break this barrier, the writer seeks the action that overwhelms this threat with experience that creates new knowledge, that alters the stakes, the risk, and the needs of the character.

How does the writer probe the play's middle like a cook who sticks a wire in a cake to test if it is done? Is it gooey and soft, still raw and ready to collapse into unconnected bits, tasty though they may be? We could ask the writer, but the writer is as full of rationalizations as the patient. Better to ask the characters. If you haven't done something like this already, ask the character, "Who the hell are you? Describe yourself, all of you: your secret self, your cleaned-up-for-your-parents self, your physical self, your obsessed fantasizing self, your oppressed self, your freed self, along with what shames you, excites you, and what you can't do without? What about your dog, sex, carrots, coffee, TV, your electric toothbrush, your car, your mom? In other words, what is your story?" Ask plenty. Ask what significant actions the character fears, actions that are destructive, such as, keeping silent or uninvolved when she wants the opposite or pretending she is someone she is not. Ask the character what are the three things most necessary to her life. Ask the character to take one away until only one is left, and tell why she takes each away.

Armed Resistance

We can disagree over how, but a story must end. For the writer, the certainty of the end, along with the expectation of change or its fraught denial, energizes the narrative landscape. Just as the patient resists giving up the repetitions of the past, the writer often resists the demands of the end. We resist things that are hard to do; we put them off, thinking the answer will come. The end of a story can offer too many choices, and yet, no right choice presents itself. We are unsure what completes the emotional form of the story. The writer can look over a shoulder and start judging the play's choices as too positive, not tough enough, too serious or not serious enough, too mainstream, too edgy. Then you're no longer writing your play, you're marketing it.

You can grow middle flab. You just keep disgorging words blindly, thinking their sheer weight will break through or overflow the barrier of the end. You think, "The characters will figure this out if I just stay out of the way." Maybe not. What if the characters need to stay lost? What if they fear the end as much as the writer? Then you think, "After all this work, I can't go back and start over." You are like the hiker who wasn't paying attention and took the wrong trail. You either can decide to go back and find the right trail or get lost. Forget it, it's too far back, it will take too much time. Is this when you should ask whether writing is the life for you? There is a powerful inertia that takes over once a certain critical mass of text is in place. This is a major risk in endings. We can make choices that are in no way connected to any real emotional form that undergirds the characters. The story can collapse on itself, becoming just one thing after another, or a narrative can suddenly stop as if the power went out. Or as I've heard Mac Wellman (an influential writer and teacher at Brooklyn College, City University of New York) advise the lost, just drive the play over the cliff: at least you'll have the thrill of a sudden change of direction.

The writer resists because some things in the text cause emotional pain and anxiety. The story is attached to the writer like the dream is attached to the dreamer. The nearer we come to the losses of our own lives, the greater our anxiety. We respond with the dodging and feinting that are the signs of denial and conflict. Emotional demands can create character changes that are credible when experienced in the event. The opposite of this is to push changes onto the character without credible discoveries for the character and the audience.

What Do You Want?

How important is the work of rewriting? It may not be quite right but . . . A lot of good stuff is there: pithy, funny, poignant, flashes of poetry even. What are you after anyway? Brooks says of the reader, "[T]he death of the ending quickens meaning: death in narrative [as in the end is the death of the story] . . . is the "flame" at which we as readers, solitary and forlorn because cut off from meaning, warm our "shivering" lives (*Reading for the Plot*, 96).

You didn't know the reader was so desperate, did you? What about the writer? Why would the writer want anything different than what the reader wants? If there is no flame at the end "by which to warm yourself," it doesn't matter whether you believe in Aristotle, Brecht, Chekhov, Beckett, or none of the above, or in the coherence of character, or the possibility of knowing or doing. The writer has to decide whether there is a flame, and so will the actor and audience.

Can you lose an ending? Is it like losing your keys, your dog, your past? Hélène Cixous in *Three Steps on the Ladder of Writing* speaks of the impact on the writer of losing an ending.

> As an author I can say that if we are accidentally seized with worry about a text's ending then this is a totally peculiar experience, one that is disturbing and not necessarily agreeable. If we are completely lost we ask ourselves: How will this end? Will it end? And what if it doesn't end? This question can take hold of you. It's far more upsetting than the question of beginning. For one thing a text can have begun before us, which is the best way. For another, getting stuck with the beginning—an experience I have never had—is not so serious since we only have to wait. The text will end up by beginning. A text that

> presents itself but doesn't end questions the identity of what we are doing. But does a dream end? Perhaps we don't think about it much since it's a difficult moment. The fact that the end might escape us is perhaps the sensation we find most difficult to reconcile with. If the end escapes us where are we? (98)

Endings are not formulas; they are organic to the world of the writer. To lose an ending is a sign the writer has lost the crucial connection to the emotional form of the work. But how do we deal with Cixous' question: Where are we if we lose the end? The end is a pressure point in the process.

Practice: Atom Smashing

A way forward for the writer in this case is what I call atom smashing. Modern physics happily engages in the destruction of invisible particles by smashing them into each other at tremendous speeds to discover the flavors of energy that lies hidden within. A little smashing is in order to take the writer and the character past the resistance generated by the search for an end. Hurl a colliding force at your character without thinking too much: a lie, a terrible misunderstanding, a betrayal, deceit, temptation, a gesture of cruelty whether intended or not. Then sift through the debris for what was hidden that you didn't see before. This collision event may or may not end up in your play. You may find that the process of deciding what atom or event to smash already has shifted the landscape.

Embrace the Mess

Schlueter quotes Samuel Beckett, who made the task of the modern artist, "To find a form that accommodates the mess" (59). Dramatic action is created by the psychodynamics of human behavior. Emotional form is the convergence of the writer's present and past with the fictional stand-ins of character and narrative event. Plot is the body of emotional form. The nervous system of emotional form arises from character. Character is fractured and disrupted by a binding conflict. The past binds the character to the trouble of the present. Weak and strong forces are mixed in conflicted behavior. Unchecked, the strong forces have the power to destroy. But they also have the power to transform or when unchanged, have the power to imprison. The beauty of dramatic texts is that they may break from a linear causality, engage in poetic or rhetorical jumps, or locate the action in an abstract or fantastic world, as long as they still express authentic human behavior.

Knowing Life from Death: Pinter's *Birthday Party*

Harold Pinter's *Birthday Party* provides a provocative example of the fracturing and disruption of a character by a binding conflict that, when unchecked, holds the power to destroy. It shows emotional form operating outside the stylistics of realism and engaging the Beckettian task of finding a form to accommodate the mess. Pinter's choice doesn't diminish the shaping force of emotional form; in fact, it makes its application even more necessary.

In the final act of *The Birthday Party,* Pinter creates an exchange between Goldberg and McCann, characters who mysteriously appear and disrupt the status quo of the central character, Stanley. This exchange can be read as a description of the writer's process of ending. McCann and Goldberg are waiting, bags packed. McCann starts tearing the morning paper into strips. He has done this earlier in the play, and he won't explain what he's doing or allow anyone to touch his torn strips. Goldberg snaps at him.

GOLDBERG: Stop doing that!
MCCANN: What?
GOLDBERG: Why do you do that all the time? It's childish, it's pointless. It's without a solitary point.
MCCANN: What's the matter with you today?
GOLDBERG: Questions, questions. Stop asking me so many questions. What do you think I am? (85)

A newspaper is a selected coherence of the random discontinuity of everyday life. McCann (or the writer) resists the coherence presented by the newspaper. The "news of the day" can never represent human meaning in the passage of time because it doesn't know the hidden order, the hidden meaning. McCann's obstinate deconstruction doesn't put the separated parts into any new order that will create a meaning. No, this is the purpose of endings. Goldberg's irritable outburst at seeing yet another set of news strips is the anger at empty endings. In the division of labor between these characters, it is Goldberg who is in charge of the end. He organizes the events that have dislodged Stanley from his "news of the day." Goldberg has been the image of competent vitality in the play. Now he is suddenly unable to act, like the writer who experiences a sudden loss of assurance and decisiveness, it is a holding back when facing the end.

What rouses Goldberg from his lethargic resistance? It is the expression of blind, furious emotion. McCann calls him a name only Goldberg's wife and mother called him. He screams at McCann not to call him by that name. Goldberg acts as if something intimate, of enormous human value, was violated. Now in motion, Goldberg struggles with what he believes. He retreats to tradition and the wisdom of his dying father and his vow to live by his father's precepts.

> GOLDBERG: . . . I swore on the good book. And I know the word I had to remember—Respect! Because McCann—(*Gently.*) Seamus—who came before your father? His father. And who came before him? Before him? . . . (*Vacant—triumphant.*) Who came before your father's father but your father's father's mother! Your great-gran-granny. (88)

There is about endings something old and unshakeable that doesn't ask for our acceptance. Endings play on our emotional need, our feelings of awe and loyalty to a deep past when great Enders roamed the earth. Accept it. Tradition says, "This is how you'll be judged, like it or not, otherwise you'll be a nothing, a schnorrer."

Then Goldberg does something surprising. Something that feels ancient, intimate, sexual and irrational, and just as he appears certain, ready to, "finish the bloody thing." He says to McCann, "All the same, give me a blow. (*Pause.*) Blow in my mouth." MCCANN *stands, puts his hands on his knees, bends, and blows in* GOLDBERG*'s mouth.* "One for the road." *McCann blows again in his mouth.* GOLDBERG *breathes deeply, smiles.* "Right!" (89).

It is commonly said of an ending that it "took my breath away." Do we mean it nearly made me faint and lose who and where I am, or do we mean it took my breath because it gave me such a jolt of energy, as if I'd been sleepwalking? Our breath is taken away in moments of realization, ecstasy, completion, surrender, and beauty. We lose our breath in moments of fear, loss, struggle, and flight. Perhaps endings are a science of breath.

Pinter keeps Stanley's conflict as opaque as a Kafka mystery. Two authority-laden strangers visit an ordinary schmo. They accuse him of being a human failure. At the end, they take him away. The strangers' motives are not explained. The fear they invoke in Stanley blossoms like a Rorschach blot. What appears as abstract, or elusive, or symbolic in the play is propelled by a cold ferocity whose impact is comic and disturbing. Pinter challenges us to connect the end to the beginning and to understand the change.

Who are these strangers? Are they functionaries of a monolithic state removing the failures from our midst? Are they henchmen hired by a powerful but unrevealed, corrupt family? Or are they part of Stanley's mind? How do we find an end when Stanley stops talking two-thirds through the play? What happens is intense and fluid, like a dream. The way to understand a dream and emotional form is the same: follow the affect.

The Birthday Party tells the story of Stanley Webber and takes place in a boardinghouse in a seaside town. A husband and wife, Petey and Meg, are the proprietors. Petey has a deck-chair concession on the boardwalk, while Meg runs the house. She is cheerful and self-absorbed. She has formed an eroticized mothering relationship with their boarder Stanley, now in his mid-thirties. He is a piano player and may have briefly held a job on the pier. The mystery of their boarder begins early in the play when Meg engages in sexualized game-playing as she rouses Stanley to come for breakfast. The situation of a sedate older couple prattling away at breakfast becomes a puzzle. Why is Meg behaving as she does with their boarder, and why is he behaving like a slouchy teenage son?

MEG: I'm going to call him. (*She goes to the door.*) Stan! Stanny! (*She listens.*) Stan! I'm coming up to fetch you if you don't come down! I'm coming up! I'm going to count three! One! Two! Three! I'm coming to get you! (*She exits and goes upstairs. In a moment, shouts from Stanley, wild laughter from Meg. Petey takes his plate to the hatch. Shouts. Laughter. Petey sits at the table silence. She returns.*) He's coming down. (*She is panting and arranges her hair.*) I told him if he didn't hurry up he'd get no breakfast. (23–24)

When Stanley appears, "He is unshaven, in his pajama jacket and wears glasses." He has been stuck in this boardinghouse for some time, jobless, directionless, and idling in the mothering attentions of Meg and the passive acceptance of Petey.

Stanley and Meg joke and tease one another. Stanley calls the fried bread she just served him succulent.

MEG: You shouldn't say that word.
STANLEY: What word?
MEG: That word you said.
STANLEY: What, succulent—?
MEG: Don't say it!
STANLEY: What's the matter with it?
MEG: You shouldn't say that word to a married woman. (27)

Meg ruffles Stanley's hair. He picks up the paper and says, as if it is in the news, "I don't know what I'd do without you." He puts up a fuss about how bad her tea is. Meg asks shyly, "Am I really succulent?" The surface of this banter can turn abruptly.

STANLEY: Oh, you are. I'd rather have you than a cold in the nose any day.
MEG: You're just saying that.
STANLEY: (*Violently.*) Look, why don't you get this place cleared up! It's a pigsty. And another thing, what about my room? It needs sweeping. It needs papering. I need a new room!
MEG: (*Sensual, stroking his arm.*) Oh, Stan, that's a lovely room. I've had some lovely afternoons in that room. (*He recoils from her in disgust, stands and exits quickly by the door on the left.*) (29)

Stanley's flirtatious language and Meg's response arise from below the neck. With Meg, Stanley's language is roiled by an unfiltered aggression. Soon we see that his aggression is entangled in some past threat linked to his father. We learn about this threat when Meg asks when he will play the piano again. His answer points to loss and shame in his past. It festers and arrests his will.

> I had a unique touch. Absolutely unique. . . . My father nearly came down to hear me. Well, I dropped him a card anyway. But I don't think he could make it. No, I—I lost the address, that was it. (*Pause.*) . . . Then after that, you know what they did? They carved me up. Carved me up. It was all arranged, it was all worked out. My next concert. Somewhere else it was. In winter. I went down there to play. Then, when I got there, the hall was closed, the place was shuttered up, not even a caretaker. They'd locked it up. (*Takes off his glasses and wipes them on this pajama jacket.*) A fast one. They pulled a fast one. I'd like to know who was responsible for that. (*Bitterly.*) All right, Jack, I can take a tip. They want me to crawl down on my bended knees. Well I can take a tip . . . any day of the week. (32–33)

Stanley's speech boils up from below the neck as a stew of resentment and fear attached to his father. The story is the only explanation we have of what led Stanley to hide in the boarding house. The volatility of Stanley's feelings for Meg shows he is in untenable compromise with the pressure from a churning conflict.

The character Lulu knocks at the door. As a young and available woman, her encounter with Stanley brings into focus the picture of Stanley's conflict. Invited to go out, he is frozen but blurts out absurd wishes.

STANLEY: (*Abruptly.*) How would you like to go away with me?
LULU: Where?
STANLEY: Nowhere. Still, we could go.
LULU: But where could we go?
STANLEY: Nowhere. There's nowhere to go. So we could just go. It wouldn't matter.
LULU: We might as well stay here.
STANLEY: No. It's no good here.
LULU: Well, where else is there?
STANLEY: Nowhere.
LULU: Well, that's a charming proposal. (36)

With her sexual air, Lulu promises a little dalliance, but Stanley rebuffs unless she is willing to flee unquestioningly to nowhere. Funny and disturbing at once, it appears to be where he is. He clings to mother Meg but won't venture a relationship with a woman his age. He has fled from the world of the adult, unwilling to risk love.

Stanley is transfixed by something in his past and by conflicted feelings about his potency in the world. The closer he comes to the mothering Meg, the angrier and more paralyzed he gets. At the beginning of the play, the galaxy of his conflict includes mother, father, and an arrested sexuality. He appears a likeable, cranky, schmo, fallen from some catastrophe and existentially unable to move. He is deeply ignorant of the forces contending in his life.

Two men come to Meg and Petey's boardinghouse, not by accident but deliberately to find Stanley: an older man named Goldberg and his younger assistant McCann. Stanley fears and resists them. They proceed to take over the events in the boardinghouse by insisting on a birthday celebration for Stanley. Out of the blue, they accuse him of a comically long list of sins without explaining who they are or how they know him. They join in celebrating Stanley's birthday. During a game of blind man's bluff, Stanley assaults Meg and the pretty neighbor, Lulu. Goldberg and McCann seize control of Stanley. In the final act of the play, Stanley appears shaved, dressed in a suit. He is taken away after the two men recite another comic litany, but this one lists the things they will do to help him. Two-thirds through the play, the central character has stopped talking.

In the final moments, Stanley only utters incoherent sounds before being taken away. How does emotional form work to shape an end in such a play?

Are Goldberg and McCann figures of judgment who find people who live outside tradition so they can rebirth them, Beckett-fashion, into the grave of a new conformity? Or are they dream-like figures lodged in Stanley's own mind, actors of his deepest wishes and fears? Emotional form picks the second option as the strangers personify the forces contending in Stanley, remaining undefined and unmoored in an objective reality. Thus, the energy of the play jumps out of Stanley's paralysis and aggression. Pinter has turned emotional form inside out. Goldberg and McCann have been yanked out of Stanley's mind to act on him. They are a device of art but rooted in the conflicted emotional reality of the character. It is as if Stanley's character split due to an inner pressure to become embodied as the two strangers who will not succumb to his flight from the world. The fight that ensues exposes the threat and desperation that will lead to mysterious and profound change.

Goldberg brings a patriarchal assurance and a bonhomie opposed to Meg's maternal hold on Stanley. McCann brings aggression and a thuggish intransigence. The arc of the play is Stanley's shocking transformation from the shabby, lost, furiously conflicted man unable to leave Meg's mothering world into a clean-shaven adult in a business suit unable to speak except in sounds made by infants. Interpretations of the play read this change as negative, as menacing, as Kafka-esque. Yet, they also recognize that Stanley, if left in the womby embrace of Meg, is living a kind of death.

Pinter's strangers break into Stanley's reality to effect change. Stanley's drama raises the question whether all serious personal change creates a kind of death. Change is instinctively resisted as it is fundamentally attached to loss. The key events in Stanley's struggle with change are: the appearance of Goldberg and McCann, their "fantastic" verbal attack on Stanley, Stanley's resistance in the birthday party and the game of blind man's bluff, and the mysterious transformation revealed in the departure of the "new" Stanley.

Goldberg's patriarchy insists on the power of the social order. He is a font of childhood memories, the happy events of youth, the things he learned from his father and his uncle. Goldberg, in contrast to the jumpy and brutish McCann, is expansive, relaxed, confident. Pinter nods to our sense that these two men exist only because they come from Stanley's inner world. McCann wants Goldberg to tell him what their job is. Why did they come? Goldberg answers in vague, bureaucratic terms: "The main issue is a singular issue and quite distinct from your previous work. Certain elements, however, might well approximate in points of procedure to some of your other activities" (40). This nonsense satisfies McCann but is Pinter's way of telling us, "You will have to decide by seeing what happens in the play." By giving them no real place in an external world, Pinter places them in the world below the neck. They act in the audience's emotional landscape like figures in a dream.

Goldberg's golden memories act as the male counterpart to Meg. Her eroticized affection for Stanley is countered by Goldberg's distant and rule-driven persona, confident of the right way to live. Goldberg is the exegete of good order and care of family. The first words Stanley hears from Goldberg are his praise of Meg as a "Mother in a million." Goldberg tells of his memory of parting from a girlfriend with a "little kiss on the cheek." He speaks of the chasteness of the time; she was a Sunday school teacher. He finishes in a flourish of Hallmark feeling that verges on satire.

> So I'd give her a peck and I'd bowl back home. Humming away I'd be, past the children's playground. I'd tip my hat to the toddlers, I'd give a helping hand to a couple of stray dogs, everything came natural. I can see it like yesterday. The sun falling behind the dog stadium. Ah! (53)

But Stanley fears the strangers. Who are they, what do they want, how long will they stay, why do they want to celebrate his birthday? He insists it isn't his birthday. When Meg gives him a toy drum as a present, she asks for a kiss. "His shoulders sag, he bends and kisses her on the cheek." He puts the drum around his neck.

> Taps it gently with the sticks, then marches round the table, beating it regularly. Meg, pleased watches him. Still beating it regularly, he begins to go round the table a second time. Halfway round the beat becomes erratic, uncontrolled. Meg expresses dismay. He arrives at her chair, banging the drum, his face and the drumbeat now savage and possessed. (46)

This scene ends act 1. Stanley's aggressive and regressive drumming signals his resistance to this expanded parental order of Meg and Goldberg.

Characters resist change, fear it, and bargain with those who represent it. Stanley will have none of Goldberg's bonhomie and warns, "Don't mess me about." They tell Stanley to sit and begin to accuse him. What follows is 107 lines of a dreamlike *j'accuse* by Goldberg and McCann that illuminate Stanley's self-loathing in a comically surreal court in his mind.

They hurl charges at him. He is wasting everybody's time, not bathing, not washing his dishes, killing his wife, playing a dirty game, leaving his bride at the church, changing his name, neglecting his prayers, not knowing whether the number 846 is possible or necessary, being a lecher, contaminating womankind, not paying the rent, picking his nose, being a traitor to the cloth, not knowing whether the chicken or the egg came first. STANLEY SCREAMS. They continue to accuse him of being a plague, betraying his land, his class. They conclude by declaring,

> What makes you think you exist? You're dead. You're dead. You can't live, you can't think, you can't love. You're dead. You're a plague gone bad. There's no juice in you. You're nothing but an odor. *Silence. They stand over him. He is crouched in the chair. He looks up slowly and kicks* GOLDBERG *in the stomach.* (62)

This is a comic and horrifying litany of charges. The final charge strikes us as true. It is an explosion of anxiety and guilt that demonstrates Stanley's lack of hold on the world. It combines the ridiculous, a dream-like dissection of Stanley, with stinging truth. Stanley tries to answer their accusations, but his answers dwindle and then burst out in his scream. Here are the last real words he speaks in the play.

GOLDBERG: Why did you change your name?
STANLEY: I forgot the other one.
GOLDBERG: What is your name now?
STANLEY: Joe Soap.
GOLDBERG: Speak up, Webber. Why did the chicken cross the road?
STANLEY: He wanted to—he wanted to—he wanted to . . .
MCCANN: He doesn't know.
GOLDBERG: Why did the chicken cross the road?
STANLEY: He wanted . . .
MCCANN: He doesn't know. He doesn't know which came first!
GOLDBERG: Which came first?
MCCANN: Chicken? Egg? Which came first?
GOLDBERG AND MCCANN: Which came first? Which came first? Which came first?
STANLEY: *Screams.* (61–62)

Stanley can no longer manage his inner conflict. His inner fears have broken into his hiding place with a vengeance. These are forces born of conflict and failed desire, forces that challenge Stanley's crumbling identity. The accusations erupt like a storm wrecking Stanley's tenuous hold on an identity. The attack separates Stanley from all but the most primitive defense. He holds a chair over his head as a club and a roof. Everything has shifted in his character. Is something coming to an end, or is something being born?

Stanley's retreats to silence, caught between the seductive, affectionate language of the mother, Meg, and the rule-driven, optimistic, and controlling vitality of the father, Goldberg. Each creates a distortion in Stanley's character. Meg's mixture of affection and sexuality infantilizes and paralyzes Stanley. Goldberg's cold vitality terrifies him. Stanley's response at the party is to act out his anger and rebellion against this vise.

Meg suggests the game of blind man's bluff. The game plays on the meaning of sight—something McCann acknowledges by breaking Stanley's glasses during the game. When Stanley is blindfolded, he moves toward Meg and chokes her. McCann and Goldberg rush in to throw him off. The room goes black. In the dark, there is a ratatattat on the drum; Lulu screams and faints. McCann finds a flashlight. Pinter's stage directions describes the scene.

> *McCann finds the torch on the floor, shines it on the table and Stanley. Lulu is lying spread-eagled on the table, Stanley bent over her. Stanley, as soon as the torchlight hits him, begins to giggle. Goldberg and McCann move towards him. He backs, giggling, the torch on his face. They follow him upstage, left. He backs against the hatch, giggling. The torch draws closer. His giggle rises and grows as he flattens himself against the wall. Their figures converge upon him.* (75–76)

This is the curtain of act 2. The bluffer giggles: game's up. What is the game? Deny his accusers; show them some cheek; get the girls; play the man. Throttle mom. Show dad and screw his girl? Lulu and Goldberg have been dallying throughout the party. Is this a fantasy of rebellion? Don't take me seriously; it is all a joke. Or has the flashlight caught him giggling at their upset? He can do something.

Escaping the Gooey Middle

We come to the end. Stanley is brought down from his bedroom, "dressed in a dark well cut suit and white collar. He holds his broken glasses in his hand. He is clean shaven." They look at him and start a litany of what they'll do for him. This is the opposite in tone and intent from what they did when they accused Stanley, but it is similar in style. They rattle off a comically contradictory list of things they will do for him:

GOLDBERG: Bake you cakes.
MCCANN: Help you kneel on kneeling days.
GOLDBERG: Give you a free pass.
MCCANN: Take you for constitutionals.
GOLDBERG: Give you hot tips.

. . . .

GOLDBERG: All on the house.
MCCANN: That's it.
GOLDBERG: We'll make a man of you.
MCCANN: And a woman.

. . . .

GOLDBERG: You'll be adjusted.
MCCANN: You'll be our pride and joy.
GOLDBERG: You'll be a mensch.
MCCANN: You'll be a success. (93)

At the end, they ask Stanley what he thinks. They urge him to respond. Stanley finally speaks, not in words but sounds, and finally a sound that is a word. Pinter describes Stanley as making a great effort to speak. He tries and fails then finally says, "Uh-gug . . . uh-gug . . . eeehhh-gag . . . Caah . . . caahh. . . ." They keep asking what he wants to say. In response to their urging, he repeats the sound. They still don't understand. Stanley stops trying. They take him away.

Stanley's first attempt at language after the rebellion in blind man's bluff is to say "caca, shit." He answers Goldberg in the speech of an infant. New life begins with shit, and no one should pretend otherwise. The fantastic list of things they'll do to help Stanley have given Stanley a shorthand for functioning in the world. The conflict between Meg's paralyzing affection and Goldberg's cold vitality is a given: the shit Stanley must work through if he is to live in the world.

What begins in the end? What has changed and is gone is Stanley's paralysis, his hiding like a grub in Meg's house. The "strangers" assaulted Stanley's identity, driving it to its deepest personal place where language forms out of the shit of existence. The raging interior portrait of Stanley and his resistance is what the middle of the play made visible. Suzan-Lori Parks likes the middle. She doesn't believe the writer should only think of a play as a clean forward progression where one thing leads to another, the linear mantra so many writers rebel against. In her essay "From Elements of Style," in *The America Play and Other Works*, she writes of how "Repetition and Revision" create a new basis for structure.

> "Repetition and Revision" is a concept integral to the Jazz esthetic in which the composer or performer will write or play a musical phrase once and again and again; etc.—with each revisit the phrase is slightly revised. . . . Characters refigure their words and through a refiguring of language show us that they are experiencing their situation anew. Secondly, a text based on the concept of repetition and revision is one with breaks from the text which we are told to write—the text which cleanly ARCS. . . . In such plays we are not moving from A to B but rather, for example, from A to A to A to B to A. Through such movement we refigure A. And if we continue to call this movement FORWARD PROGRESSION, which I think it is, then we refigure the idea of forward progression. And if we insist on calling writings structured with this in mind PLAYS, which I think they are, then we've got a different kind of dramatic literature. (8–10)

Repetition is at the heart of conflict. The core of the writer's dilemma is resistance to forward motion. The writer must grapple with a character pulled backwards by memory and forwards by desire, inscribing repetitive patterns that must be escaped to create the conditions for change and progress.

The end of Pinter's play may well contain a critique of a corrupt, paternalistic society, but we see Stanley facing a new beginning and feel the connection to our own search for self. The crisis in such a search requires the discovery of new language. If Stanley is bluffing this time, it is the same bluff we all make, all dressed up to enter the world.

Pinter's play can be read independent of emotional form. The reader might say there is no place to hide from a relentless state demanding crippling conformity. Such a reading lacks satisfaction, and it fails to make Stanley's behavior credible. It doesn't recognize the power in the play that reveals character and connects an audience to its own anxious dreams of threatening voices. Emotional form points to content in conflict that is obvious from the opening moments, when Meg and Stanley play house. To see the play as an abstraction of henchmen from a menacing state, one must impose that story on the progress of the narrative. The moment Stanley stops speaking, he has just attacked Meg, the mother figure, and Lulu, the sensual siren. Stanley's behavior is unambiguously psychological, sexualized, and transgressive. He has not been made mute by the state but by the collapse of his defenses against acting in the drama of his own mind.

The play is an example of emotional form as the art of the ending. Pinter shows the writer the power of a binding conflict to arrest a character. Pinter also shows how emotional form acts poetically on the evolving narrative, shaping a world and determining an ending. We don't imagine Stanley in his suit struggling to speak at the beginning. When we see Stanley in his suit, we can't understand it without recalling the beginning and his confrontation by the strangers in the middle of the play. The confrontation expands the content of the conflict Stanley describes to Meg and forces him to act. We know the link is through the trouble containing Stanley's furious, regressed behavior. Pinter engaged in atom smashing when he put Goldberg and McCann in Stanley's path. Emotional form doesn't require an explanation of the ending, but it must be aligned with the forces unleashed by the character's behavior, particularly those forces that expose the depth and mystery of human action.

Bearings: Breath and Fury

Emotional form unspools from the life and passions of the writer. This is good: the writer isn't faced with some obscure search into external sources in which the ending is hidden. After all, the writer has created the character and the content of the character's conflict out of the only material the writer knows to be true, herself. Yes, a writer does research, and, yes, a writer creates characters different from herself, but a writer is also bound to her emotional life as the lens through which she sees and feels. A writer writes from a need to expand and deepen the focus of that lens. The writer conceives of some narrative path, snips the cords binding the character, and then is faced with Goldberg's problem—full stop, looking for the inspiration of the end. Of all the vagaries the writer of a new play goes through, she has a real collaborator helping her see the rightness of the ending. Goldberg needs an assist, another's breath. That is what the writer listens for, the breath of the audience.

A writer learns from the audience, the audience of players, and the director, who actually talk back, as well as the audience who buys tickets and talks back with their responses, responses that should be read by the writer as avidly as the investor reads the portfolio details. Margulies played the game of "name that ending" partly to say to an old friend, "We know each other, let's have a little fun. We can wish and we can fear, but we both know how life works." The writer also, like Goldberg, can erupt in a fury as the forces shaping the end are deeply personal and unreachable by the energies of reason, as Master Harold discovered.

We don't write a play only for ourselves. We choose to write for the theater, a thing that exists only in partnership with an audience. In struggling with an ending, the writer is struggling with the same forces of constraint, failure, forgiveness, folly, and cruelty as the people who make up what we call the audience. They come for many reasons, but the greatest of these is to gain insight into the mystery of endings that the writer must solve. That's why they complete the live circuit among writer, performer, and perceiver. How is the audience connected to the play? How does the play connect audience and writer? What can these connections teach the writer?

4. *Collaborating with Calamity*

> However, one thing has become quite plain: the present-day world can only be described to present-day people if it is described as capable of transformation.
>
> —Bertolt Brecht, *Can the Present-Day World Be Reproduced by Means of Theatre?*

Kiss or Kill the Guests?

For the writer, there is no visibility without the audience. The relationship between audience and drama completes the circuit of emotional form among writer, text, performer, and audience. Emotional form shapes the impact and meaning of the dramatic narrative and shapes the audience's emotional experience in the theater. Artists are conflicted about the subject of the audience. They seek either to measure its receptiveness or simply dismiss it: "What do they have to do with me?"

The writer acknowledges the audience through the performer's bag of tricks that create response, the undeniable reality of box-office receipts, and the urge to eavesdrop on the chatter during intermission. Another way the audience makes itself felt is when a group of university teachers choose the plays for the new season. An anxious discussion breaks out, a mixture of anger, fear, passion, and myopia. If we listened in, we might hear: "This play is new, disturbing; it will shake up the audience." Or, "I've always wanted to do this play; I know it won't have much audience draw, but it is important." Followed by, "We don't do plays based on their popularity, do we? We don't pander to the audience." Then perhaps a sarcastic question, "Why don't people want to see the plays we want to do?"

Somewhere in this shifting discussion between high and low art, between pure and commercial is the wagging tail of an ideological dog. The signs of this ideology are such convictions as: (a) an artist lowers himself by considering the audience's needs, (b) an artist compromises his integrity by catering to popular taste, or (c) the artist's job is to raise audiences to the standards of the artist.

Artists, out of a well-earned antagonism to the mass audience and a corporatized society, can adopt a coolness to emotion as a way of resisting the sentimentality and manipulation of mass media. Remember that modernism caused a fierce fight within its new audiences, a battle between conservative traditions and progressive beliefs about the present and future of art and society. In that fight, artists heaped scorn on those resisting the vanguard, the forward rush of everything modern. Riots broke out in the theaters between the contending sides.

But it is a mistake to hold on to forms of resistance created in different times, especially if that resistance is not connected to a new campaign for a new audience. Has an uncertain audience for new plays forced the theater to downsize? New plays today are found primarily in small venues such as the Off and Off Off Broadway theaters that seat one hundred or fewer. In fact, these theaters are springing up, not the larger institutional venues. This is not only due to costs, it is as much about artists' resistance to mass culture, their flight from the commercialism of mainstream theater, and a general alienation from the values of the establishment. Is it also an indifference to what makes the society work? Suzi Gablik in *Has Modernism Failed?* argues there is "a problem of modernity—loss of belief in any system of value beyond self. . . . Modern consciousness is solitary, consequent to the disestablishing of communal reality" (31). In the age of the Internet and self-obsessed social networks, is her view still accurate?

Fighting for an Audience

Every reinvention of drama includes a reinvention of the audience. Imagining a new drama includes imagining a fight for a new audience, with a new set of beliefs about the future. That is a fight worth having. Consider the vast numbers of theater departments in U.S. public and private universities and in community colleges. If you think like a film producer, this network looks like a distribution system for new work. What is the reality of season choices in this network—probably two-thirds familiar work from the dead-writer repertory. Yet, isn't this a country that prides itself on innovation, creativity, risk taking, experimentation? Why, then, do theater departments resist the work of living writers and fail to engage their students in the quest to develop writers from around the country and the world? I heard a student attending a theater conference say she'd never been involved in the production of a new play and ask, "How do you go about it?" The disconnect between theater programs and new work creates a loss both to the students and the audience. Thus, the voices and language of new work cannot become part of learning the creative process for students, just as audiences cannot enter into the contemporary dialogue emerging from contemporary writers. These programs are creating a self-fulfilling prophecy that audiences won't come to see new work because it isn't presented to them with the confidence and frequency that allows an audience to grow. Every significant period of theater history taught by these academic programs had a vital connection to living writers. What about our period?

The audience brings us to issues about the margins and the mainstream and how and when they intersect. There is more at stake in understanding the audience than simply social profiling or box-office trends. For the writer, the audience is the proof of the connective power in a work and the reach of its emotional form. Oscar Lee Brownstein calls this connection the missing element.

> The missing element is the most fundamental: the personal engagement of the spectator in a continuous dialogue with the play. An art which operates through time must create a dialogue with its perceiver or it must fail. The canons of art are not Forms lying about in a Platonic Bureau of Standards waiting for us to get the measurements right; they lie deeply in each of us. . . . The spectator is no detached observer, and the play is not a hermetically closed object. They are mutually intrusive, the play by its design for human perception and the spectator by his imaginative participation. (*Strategies of Drama*, xvi)

So How Did You Like It?

Artist and producer want to know what the audience experiences during a performance. There is precious little discussion of this in the academic literature or in the training of theater artists. Every theater artist knows there are two fundamentally different realities: rehearsal, without the audience; and performance, with the audience present. The fault lines of a dramatic work can only be tested before an audience. It is the arena where writer, director, and actors "discover" the work. What is discovered is whether and how deeply the work penetrates the emotional life of the audience. Writers, directors, and actors can suffocate the oxygen that fuels the fire of the audience's inner life. Sometimes the writer is caught up with smart talk, ideas and topical buzz, and the director with tricks of the trade, the razzle-dazzle of stagecraft. Or an actor may withhold himself from the core of the character. What endures is this mystery called the audience.

Herbert Blau in his 1988 article "Hysteria, Crabs, Gospel, and Random Access: Ring around the Audience" describes the need for the link between audience and feeling.

> There is a sense in which the dream of community is reconstituted with every drama, in the mirror of production, but as Oedipus suggests to Theseus before the "theophany" at Colonus—where he passes

> into the pure symbolic—if the theatre attests to anything, it is to aloneness and alienation, the essential rupture in the essential drama. (10)

He writes that drama forms a dream, one that the audience sees but cannot enter. We discover our essential aloneness with this realization. One of the most successful modern American productions of Sophocles, *The Gospel at Colonus*, as staged by Lee Breuer, is set in a church before a black gospel choir. At the "death" of Oedipus, the choir breaks into a hand-clapping, foot-stomping, roof-raising hymn with the choral refrain "Raise him up" that raises the audience onto its feet singing, and clapping. The drama creates a public rapture to address the essential rupture.

First things first. Who's there? There must be a who if there is to be a connection between the emotional form of the play and an emotional inner world of a spectator. The audience does signal its response to an actor's craft of timing, to the release of building emotion, to surprise, to comedy, to displays of bravura skill. Yet, most of the time, the audience's inner experience is hidden. Despite all the postproduction discussions where audiences are invited to speak to the cast and director, we are not much closer to knowing what the audience experiences. Who is there?

And why should the writer care? Doesn't the writer have enough to do? Yes and no. The writer can't be the audience, but the way a writer views the audience does matter. Viewed with contempt, the writer may manipulate for effect or reinforce unexamined beliefs. Viewed with respect, the writer may approach the audience as equally curious, engaged in the search, serious and comic, for the truth of human experience. Some writers feel thinking about the audience is a trap and want no part of it, like overanalyzing a relationship that is better experienced than examined. Emotional form is always present in the writer's work. It is through emotional form that the audience enters and finds its deep shared connection to the work. Understanding the audience experience may also tell us something about writing.

The Secret Life of the Audience

What do people experience in a performance? What use do they make of it? Two of the most familiar approaches to this question are based in aesthetics or critical theory. The first is the concept of distance introduced by Edward Bullough in 1912. Distance is a psychic state that lets the viewer put the phenomenon of performance out of sync with the everyday self. There is a distance-limit that makes aesthetic appreciation possible. To violate this limit causes the viewer to fall out of this state and regard all before him with the cold eye of practical, selfish reality. Bullough uses the example of *Othello.* If the circumstances of the play trigger the personal, emotional response of a jealous spectator, he will lose the psychic distance necessary to experience these circumstances as a work of art. At the extreme, the spectator might break into the action on stage incited by his own jealous rage. Another theoretical view focuses on how we create meaning when we read. The audience reading a performance is subject to the same interior response as the reader confronting a text. Norman Holland in "Unity Identity Text Self" believes the key is in identity.

> [I]dentity re-creates itself. . . . That is, all of us, as we read, use the literary work to symbolize and finally to replicate ourselves. We work out through the text our own characteristic patterns of desire and adaptation. We interact with the work, making it part of our own psychic economy and making ourselves part of the literary work—as we interpret it. (124)

Both of these approaches send us to the internal landscape of the individual seated in the audience. They take seriously the psychological dimension of the audience member's connection to the fictional world of the drama, just as the theory of emotional form asks the writer to take seriously her own psychological connection to the work she is creating.

Who does occupy the seats in the theater? The audience arrives, finds seats, and looks on with anticipation as darkness engulfs the auditorium. After seeing a performance, we rarely talk about what happened to us except in terms of fast-food reviews: "He was awful; she was marvelous; the play stank; it put me to sleep; it was inspirational; the language was crude; I loved every word of it." This isn't all that happened in the two hours spent silently watching and listening. Perhaps you find it hard to talk about what you just experienced. Instead of talking, your mind clings to images, feelings, and fragments of action that can't easily be shared. The fact is most of us find it difficult to talk about our experience immediately after a performance. Why? Does this difficulty in speaking, starting and stopping, jumping about the subject, resemble the speech of lovers or children or our own confused attempts to describe our dreams?

Such difficulty results from the laws of our inner world, which is just as necessary to the artist as natural law is to the scientist. Our inner world responds to such forces as justice, power, revenge, love, fear, sex, death, freedom, and loss. This response mirrors the content the writer infuses into the characters and conflicts of the play. The political authorities of every culture recognize the power of these forces and of those who can express them or use them to incite others.

Take Oedipus live on stage, pursuing the murderer of Laius. Sophocles is not telling you about an Oedipus who once lived and suffered in a certain way. We are not told a story that can be broken off and continued another day. The audience is witness to his life and its consequences without the intermediary of a storyteller. Everyone knows that Oedipus murdered his father, married, and sired children with his mother, all in ignorance of his identity. When we watch Oedipus, in real dramatic time, discover that his wife, Jocasta, is his mother, and he is his own father's murderer, this moment of discovery unhinges the existing order. Jocasta hangs herself. Oedipus takes a pin from her dress and stabs it into his eyes.

We are sitting beside our neighbors filled with this sudden destruction of another person's world. Who are we at *that* moment? Can we say with any certainty we are so-and-so from somewhere, that we have this profession, these friends or children? The act of theater makes us forget. Under the spell of performance, we forget part of our identity. We know that people in love forget their everyday selves that take care of eating, appointments, and rational conversation. We accept that they are in touch with a deeper self. When we experience this extraordinary self, we feel profoundly human and free. We are no one at the moment of Oedipus's discovery and blinding. In that seat is a self we experience only in moments of intimacy, an intimacy that engages our deepest values and secrets but which has no name. This is the self the writer must reach.

This is why no quick answer comes to the question, "So how did you like the play?" This self has no language at the ready that describes what was just experienced. That experience was intensely private, touching on emotional events at the core of our lives called out by the emotional form of the play's narrative. The chance to reach these feelings in ourselves is what we came for; this is the contrary world of drama: real pleasure and vicarious suffering.

The audience is, as it always has been, a fundamental barometer of the success of the writer's work. Knowing this, the writer must test a new work with an audience and find a producing partner to make this happen. Readings have a place in the process of developing a new work, but there is no substitute for production. For those toiling in universities who offer to teach writers and send them into the world, it is a fundamental issue. The only way student writers can experience the audience is in production. Yet, writers can go through established graduate programs with little experience of production. This is in part because university theater training programs rarely present new works by living writers, never mind works by the writers training and working in their midst. This suggests a blindness or avoidance in the curricula of these programs, an underlying distrust of the value of work by new writers, a fetishizing of the past and its canon, and a capitulation to the self-fulfilling prophecy that audiences will not come to see new work.

So it is for the audience that the writer works and prepares nervously as for a blind date who worries that the "date" may not show up or will flee at the first chance. The writer has no way of really knowing what ticket buyers will connect to or whether they will "fall in love." The writer can only set the table. The writer prepares a mix of truth, revelation and exhilaration, surprise and a promise that the "date" drawn to the meal will profoundly "forget" her everyday self.

Catharsis—Raw or Cooked

The Greeks discovered another essential element about the audience's experience of drama. The Greeks recognized there were necessary conditions under which the audience would connect to the tragic hero. Aristotle commented on these in the *Poetics*, and we refer to them today with the word *catharsis*. A frustrated writer might object, "The Greeks? Tell me why the audience hates my character!" Unless your character is just plain boring, you will have to consider how catharsis works. Emotional form creates a bridge between the writer's work and the audience. The bridge has a tollbooth, and the token of entry is catharsis.

Gerald Else's translates the meaning of the *catharsis* passage in the *Poetics*, using the well-known terms *pity* and *fear*.

> Tragedy, then, is a process of imitating an action which has serious implications, is complete and possesses magnitude; by means of language which has been made sensuously attractive, with each of its varieties found separately in the parts; enacted by the persons themselves and not presented through narrative; through a course of pity and fear completing the purifications of tragic acts which have those emotional characteristics. (*Aristotle:* Poetics, 25)

Else argues this description attaches catharsis to the emotional reaction of the spectator (*Aristotle's* Poetics, 227). Catharsis is not a purgative or physical relief. The writer is not an emotional pharmacist. The medicinal twist we often give the term was the brainchild of the German linguist Jakob Bernays (1824–81), who saw the play thickening and stirring the emotions of the audience. These feelings come to a pitch and are released, or purged. If this is what you want from drama, take an Alka-Seltzer. It will save you the price of the ticket.

What is significant for the writer is that catharsis is tied to the "purification of tragic acts." For the Greeks, the writer achieved this "purification" through a construction of the plot that separated the pathos, the tragic consequence of the character's act, from our judgment and moral rejection of the character and the events. Such a separation allows the audience to admit the character's "tragic acts" into its own emotions, creating pity and fear. The word *purification* is alien to the modern ear. When a writer creates a character who commits a terrible act, the writer's job is to create a path for the audience to admit that character to their sympathy.

This is the most significant achievement of dramatic structure. Because of it, the Greek audience could stay involved in tragic tales about the shedding of kindred blood. In their world, the individual who shed kindred blood became polluted, an enemy of society, beyond sympathy. Society's response was to kill the perpetrator of such crimes. The furies call for this response as they pursue Orestes, who had his mother's blood on his hands.

If there is no catharsis, there is no emotional connection outside those of anger fueled by judgment. An audience that cannot admit a character and a character's actions into its feelings stops being an audience and becomes a jury. A smart defense lawyer tries to reverse this process, painting a client so the jury can move away from judgment to catharsis, transforming the guilty deeds into not-guilty judgments. Aristotle believed the writer can create a plot that will change heinous acts to tragic acts.

> First of all, so far as the plot as a whole is concerned, if it is to gain his sympathy and ultimately his fear and/or pity, he must make two judgments (one or the other, and, for the best effect, both): (1) that the hero is "like himself," and (2) that he does not deserve his misfortune. These judgments are not after-effects of the spectator's feeling, they are the prerequisites to it, the conditions which must be satisfied *before his psyche* (that is, the rational element in his soul) *will allow the emotions to be felt.* (quoted in Else, *Aristotle's* Poetics, 436)

The Greeks developed plot so tragic events became less about what was done and more about who did the deeds and how they came to be done. After all, the deeds in the myths behind the plays were universally known. The events of the plot allow us to "see" the character differently. Without the actions of the plot, he is viewed as a criminal, but within them, he becomes someone "like ourselves." The audience suspends judgment and forms an emotional sympathy with the story. They can feel themselves into the story.

All You Can Eat

The claim is that drama lies within the realm of human feeling and perception tied to the god Dionysus. The plays Aristotle discussed in the *Poetics* were presented at the Dionysia, Athens's premier theater festival. There is an aspect of the worship of Dionysus that relates to catharsis. His worshippers, the Bacchantes, are described in states of ecstatic transformation as rending and eating animals. The purpose of these acts of ritual worship was to bring the god inside. The writers of tragic drama learned to do something similar, only without the blood. The writer constructs a plot that allows the audience to take in a character in crisis—often one who threatens, defies, or undermines himself and the social order—into their inner lives as if consumed or eaten. The writer prepares the character like a dish to be served to the audience in a negotiation of judgment, feeling, and meaning. Catharsis is what the writer uses to make the meal palatable.

We can be invited to eat but not made to eat. The mind is one of our private parts, no less than the mouth. Audiences don't eat the body and the blood, as in some ritual transubstantiation. They eat the *act* of the body. The writer cooks the act. An act not separated from deliberate evil or malicious intent is inedible. The writer can prepare acts of murder and catastrophe so skillfully that we take a paradoxical pleasure in their eating. Emotional form is the discipline of conceiving and preparing dangerous acts so they satisfy an unspoken hunger in the audience.

You Said a Goat?

The power of catharsis is revealed in the ability of drama to take acts that society considers shocking or taboo and admit them to our emotional experience, suspending disgust and judgment. Edward Albee's *Goat or Who Is Sylvia?* is the work of a skillful cook who turns a forbidden food into a meal. The act that Albee makes available for consumption is that of a man literally having intercourse with an animal. When we meet Martin, his mask is in place: a husband, successful architect, and father, a solid social being. We are astonished to realize by the end of the first act that he is in love with and makes love to a goat named Sylvia. To get us to eat this act, Albee cooks it in the conflicted depth of his character Martin's love, yes, love for a goat. Although it threatens every link in the chain that anchors his life, he clings to a madness of love he cannot escape. The writer changes judgment by revealing intention. If he is "befouled" by a selfish perversion, we will judge him harshly and push the dish away, but if we see him as besotted, helpless with love, caught in a mysterious but still human action, not the gratuitous action of his loins, and paying a price for his madness, then perhaps we can be drawn to partake.

Consider an even more controversial play, Sarah Kane's *Blasted*. The play creates a landscape of human vulnerability and sexual brutality where the most common act is rape that morphs into torture and cannibalism. All this takes place in the banal setting of an upscale hotel room in which Ian, a loutish, middle-aged journalist, meets Cate, a young, simple-minded woman prone to fainting spells. These two once had some kind of relationship. Ian wears a pistol, smokes, drinks gin, hates foreigners and other races. He wants sex from Cate, who doesn't want sex with him. He is dying from lung disease and fears death. Cate has no experience of the world beyond taking care of her mother and brother and going to soccer games. She resists sex but flirts with Ian. She agrees to be in a hotel room alone with him, claims to have a boyfriend, and is angry that Ian stopped paying attention to her in the past. These are wrecked souls adrift with no compass of any kind.

Violence moves through the play in three waves. The first is against Cate. Ian makes her help him masturbate and rapes her violently so she awakens bleeding in the morning. The second is against Ian via the outside reality of war moving into the hotel room. An armed soldier enters and takes control of Ian. He plays mental games about the kind of violence of which Ian is capable. He tells stories of the brutality he has committed and of what was done to his family. He rapes Ian, then sucks out his eyeballs, and eats them. War enters the room directly as a mortar blast blows a hole in the wall. The third wave begins when Cate enters holding a baby she has found. The soldier has shot himself in the head. We might be in Bosnia, Mogadishu, Gaza, Iraq; this is a world that implicates us. It is cold, they are hungry, the baby dies. While Cate goes out to procure food with sex, Ian eats the baby. The critics hated Kane's play, but she was defended by Harold Pinter and by Edward Bond, who'd written an equally difficult play, *Saved*, in which young men and the father stone a baby in his carriage. Catharsis is not a shield against critics and the pieties of the establishment. Kane takes the Greeks at their word: catharsis is the condition of tragic imagination as the writer confronts the breaking points of the human spirit, the terrain of catastrophe. What starts as the deliberately cruel and confused need is overwhelmed by the context of a world reduced to the meanest forms of survival amidst chaotic violence. This shocking context alters our judgment of the actions of Ian and Cate.

One way in which the audience is essential to the writer is as the unseen collaborator in the emotional journey of the play. Catharsis develops through the writer's use of character and plot to open the action to feeling and to changed interpretations of human motives. Catharsis gives the writer a method for making evil or terrible events part of the dynamics of human ignorance and making events capable of understanding through the complicated dynamics of human knowing. The emotion of the character and the audience both are shaped by the interplay of these dynamics, ignorance and learning, as told by the writer. In the act are the intention and the wish. Emotional form takes shape from the writer's efforts to prepare a character's destructive act by exposing the conflicted, obdurate human need buried in that act. That need acts as a fire that burns in the character until its heat destroys resistance, come what may. Passion in drama tries to consume the bonds of conflicted fear, to overcome the repetitive actions that shield the past, freeze the present, and deny the future.

Can't Live with 'Em, Can't Live without 'Em

There is nothing holy about style. A character may sing, a character may be doubled, his inner thoughts may be spoken aloud or projected on a screen, he may interact with a puppet, or he may never break the mimetic frame. All of that is the sauce of presentation. What matters is the gathering force of the wish. The progress in a play relies on two principles. One is the catharsis that protects the central figure from a fatal condemnation by the audience, and the other is the emotional form that unites the central figure to actions that break the character loose from the past and creates experience to shape an end. The emotional form creates in the crucible of action a new experience that constructs new knowledge.

Can you read the narrative you've spun as if you were someone else? Not usefully. Instead, can you write with an understanding of the dynamic relation of storyteller to listener? Yes. Can you write with an aesthetic understanding of the impact of text and performance on the experience of the audience? Yes. Can you write because what you want to do is shock the audience? Yes. Can you write as though there were no audience? I don't believe it, but I hear it often. Can you write without ever learning from the responses of an audience? Hard to imagine; you'd be a fool.

Brecht's *Mr. Puntila and His Man Matti*

And then there is Brecht. No playwright of the twentieth century spilled more ink in theorizing about dramatic structure, the role of the audience, and the beliefs of the writer. He argued that thought, observation, and reflection came before emotion in the work of the dramatist in the new scientific age.

Brecht created in his plays and theatrical practices a way of controlling and cooling the power of emotion. One of his motivations in creating his epic theater technique was to change the relationship between audience and play. Brecht wanted the audience to be like spectators at a boxing match or sporting event: alert, critical, engaged in assessing the strengths and weaknesses of the contenders in an atmosphere where they are free to shout and smoke and drink and hold sway over an observers' arena surrounding the action. He saw the theater audiences of his time as the opposite of this. They were silent, as if in a trance, unthinking, given over to the emotions of the central character, uncritical of the fate he was sure to endure. He saw the audience drugged into a sleep by the emotional roller coaster of the main character, dimmed by the very art that he believed should shake them awake so they would take action in the world outside the theater.

To this end, he created plays that interrupted a scene's building emotion with song or comment or an abrupt change to the next scene. He arranged the stage to make it perfectly clear the audience was in a theater and not in an illusory world. His stagecraft revealed the apparatus of the stage, the mechanisms of lights, and scenery that moved the story along. He made the actor conscious of presenting the character, as if demonstrating the choices made. His fundamental skepticism about emotion has had a strong, lasting impact on the theater. His skepticism was born from his generation's reaction to the First World War, their revulsion to the hyped-up emotion of nationhood, to the false honor of militarism, to Romanticism's exaltation of self. They wanted a new dynamic language of observation stripped of emotional engagement.

Brecht's foe in his campaign against emotion in drama was Aristotle, who had structured tragedy around the central character, creating the conditions that arouse our empathy (pity and fear) and increase until the climatic scene of recognition. For Brecht, epic theater aimed to free the audience of the hypnotizing emotion of the central character. In place of empathy, he wanted judgment, critical awareness. Brecht's work succeeded in leaving a huge impact on the playwrights and theater of the twentieth century. We cannot avoid examining whether and how emotional form is present in his work. Did he create a way to slip loose from its shaping hand?

A surprising thing happens in his play *Mr. Puntila and His Man Matti*. The fierce skepticism and individuality of Brecht—part charm, part willful hedonism, part electrifying presence—here subverts his own ideological stance toward the political struggle between the master and the servant. In Puntila (the Master), emotional form asserts itself, perhaps despite Brecht's focus on shaping our judgment of the Master. Comedy unerringly attacks all forms of human rigidity. The events in the play reveal an emotional conflict that instead turns a critical eye on Matti, the servant, who fails to see and value what is human. The poet in Brecht does not suppress this conflict as it ties knowledge and emotion together.

Brecht based this play on the comedy *The Sawdust Princess* by the Finnish writer Hella Woulijoki. Brecht turns a folk comedy into a comic drama of class and emotional paralysis. Within this story of master and servant, he revisits the clash of the classes in August Strindberg's *Miss Julie*. Puntila is a divided character who, when drunk, overcomes all resistance to his wishes by the force of his vitality, his reckless generosity, and love of pleasure and of nature as well as his shame at his cold, sober self failing his more human self. When sober, he measures all things by his account ledger and self-interest, treating others with contempt if they threaten his purposes.

The dynamic of the master-servant relationship is about something more than class relations or harsh economic reality; it is also the expression of a psychological necessity. In Brecht's play is a cruel dialectic between boundless need and boundless weakness, both of which are found on both sides of this divide. Brecht's dramatic strategy is to put in the path of his Puntila the dispassionate and cautious Matti. Who is stronger in this master-servant divide, and what good is their strength to anyone? How is this dramatic test of strength shaped by emotional form?

When Matti meets Puntila's daughter Eva, the play views the class struggle through the sexual tensions between Eva and the cool and careful servant. Eva is entangled in her desire. She is ambivalent over her father's wish that she marry the anemic attaché Eino Silakka. Matti suggests they row out to a nearby island and catch crayfish for her engagement party the next day. A sly tug of war begins between the pretense of fishing and her real desire to go with this man, at night, to the island. Eva resolves it by stating flatly she's not marrying the attaché. She'll have Matti instead. Matti counters that marriage of mistress to servant fails because the master-servant relationship is not altered by marriage. Matti's resistance to Eva has a chauvinistic, defensive quality. He claims his awareness of their differences is truer than hers and her naiveté is vaguely beneath his contempt. Eva storms off: "No, you'd want to be the master. I can picture how you'd treat a woman . . . I just can't stand the sight of you any longer, and I hate egoists, I hate them!" (51).

The pressure on Matti to treat his role as servant as variable comes from past fits of generosity by the erratic Puntila and now from the master's daughter. Does Brecht present this change as social critique, an abuse of power, or an emotional form that raises the possibility of inner change in which risk, feeling, and courage are needed because reason or ideology are not enough?

This issue comes to a head in scene 9 (of the play's twelve scenes), entitled "Puntila Betrothes His Daughter to a Human Being." Eva has gone ahead with the engagement party during which Puntila proceeds to get drunk, becomes furious at the insipid character of the attaché, and chases him out of his house. Most of the guests clear out, and Puntila announces, "It has long been my ambition to betroth my daughter to a first-rate human being, Matti Altonen" (68).

Puntila's grandiose announcement solidifies the question of whether Matti will break loose from his servant role by learning how to change his condition or stay in his place despite his outward show of resisting Puntila. Because Puntila is drunk, his gesture is dangerous and unreal. The shift to danger is felt as the world around Eva becomes increasingly vulgar. Puntila begins his celebration of his new wedding plan by asking:

PUNTILA: Matti, can you fuck decently?
MATTI: I'm told so.
PUNTILA: That's nothing can you do it indecently? (*Eva, taking a drink, makes her declaration to Matti.*)
EVA: Dear Matti, I beseech you make me your wife so I may have a husband like other girls do, and if you like we can go straight off to catch crayfish without nets. I don't consider myself anything special despite what you think, and I can live with you even if we have to go short. (70)

Matti has to navigate what is authentic: Eva's response to him or his fears. Matti's answer is to give her a test. She is to pretend they are married and attempt to act appropriately as a chauffeur's wife in a series of situations. There are several tests: how to act when Matti has a hole in his sock; how to greet Matti when he arrives home from work; how to respond when Matti is called in the middle of the night to drive his master. In each of the test situations, Eva behaves according to her feeling for Matti. She responds with affection, running to kiss him when he comes home; she talks to him animatedly when he is reading his newspaper; she tells off the Master, who calls for him, refusing to awaken her husband after a hard day's work. She fails his test. The correct behavior is to cut out any "intimacies and lovey-dovey" when he comes home, to immediately hand him a towel so he can wash, to pull his boots off, to give him his paper without talking to him, and to wake him without fuss when the master calls. She is to mirror her husband's servility to his master. If Eva tells off the pretend master, Matti says, she'll win his mother's heart, but he'll lose his job.

The next moment is a surprise and darkens the comic sequence we've just seen. Matti laughs over her feisty refusal to wake him to drive the master and slaps Eva on the ass.

EVA: (*Speechless, then furious.*) Stop that at once.
MATTI: What's the matter?
EVA: How dare you hit me there? (*The Judge has stood up, touches Eva on the shoulder.*)
JUDGE: I'm afraid you failed your test after all, Eva.
EVA: And I now see my education was all wrong. I think I'll go upstairs. (76–77)

After this exit, Eva is never seen again.

In typical comic dramaturgy, Eva has been taught a lesson that overthrows her old beliefs about men and women, one that shows what love, and not the romanticized version, means in the working classes. However, unlike traditional comic learning that transforms and expands her ability to relate and deepens her love, this lesson is cynical, and the opposite occurs. Eva brings flexibility to the situation, but instead of overthrowing an old rigidity, she is perversely forced to accept a new rigidity in which she must deny feelings and create as much subservience to a working-class mate as she would have in the empty, respectable marriage to the limp attaché. Matti protects the shame that is associated with his place. He cannot bluster and rage like his master. He quietly projects his weakness outward by his test of Eva. Yet, the aggression this weakness masks assumes a sexual familiarity he hasn't earned emotionally.

Matti is controlled by a desire for subservience. His desire is to serve, not in the religious sense, humbling himself for the good of the world, but rather in the sense of servility, humbling himself before power. When Brecht wrote this play in 1940, he already knew that Stalin's NKVD was wrecking the promise of communism through demands for slavish obedience to the dictator's paranoia and by the murder of all dissent. Perhaps this is why this conflict in Matti is untethered from Brecht's usual critique of power and class, a perspective that would limit the emotional meaning. What Matti does in the engagement scene is to report himself to the authorities like a sycophantic party spy trying to save his skin: "See, I am really not a human being because what I am is the very embodiment of weakness, the very thing you hate, a creature so servile he cannot allow even love to alter his servility." In giving Eva the test, Matti simultaneously teaches Puntila what he, Matti, really is: a creature of fear.

The Lesson of Imagination

Brecht deals with this fear, a fear that has disturbed the comic surface of the play, by confronting the emotional underpinnings of master and servant instead of critiquing the social conditions of the world. The play's finale shifts the battle of class defined as battle of the sexes to a battle for Matti's soul. The next day, Puntila, upset that he banished the wealthy suitor, resolves to smash his liquor supply. Yet, he winds up drunk as he tastes each bottle before breaking it. First, he blames Matti for all his troubles, then dreamily raises his salary, "Because I'm particularly pleased with you." He announces he wants to climb Mount Hatelma with Matti "so I can show you what a splendid country you live in, you'll kick yourself for not realizing it earlier." Matti answers, "I'll do whatever you fancy, any day of the week" (88).

Puntila quickly replies, "I wonder if you have the imagination." Matti is silent. This question resonates not only in this play but also throughout Brecht's commentaries on the theater. Does Matti have the imagination to see himself outside the embrace of Puntila, free of the heel of obedience and silence? Do we have the imagination to see the world as alterable, changeable, and able to reject what diminishes human worth? Puntila orders, "Make me a mountain" (88).

Now Matti is tested. At first, the test seems a simple game of make-believe. Matti "makes" the mountain by kicking apart a gun locker and a grandfather clock and piling the debris together with some chairs on top of Puntila's billiard table. They climb. After they reach the "summit," Puntila begins an ecstatic recitation of the beauty he can see, stopping at the break in each stanza of his panegyric to ask Matti whether he, too, can see it. He rhapsodizes about the smells. He compares the summer air to the haze of love, adding, "I don't think you get that kind of love outside Tavastland either" (90).

Matti replies, "Where I was born we used to have caves with rocks outside them round as cannon balls polished all over" (90). Together, they imagine cows swimming across the lake. The maids enter, and he asks Matti to join them in a verse, "And the waves on the beautiful Roina / Are kissing the milky-white sand" (91).

What is Puntila's test? It is to see if Matti can express the unironic, uncunning feeling that reveals pleasure in nature and love that Puntila embraces at the top of Mount Hatelma. Matti makes the first step when he shares with Puntila his memory of the caves of his boyhood and then joins him in "seeing" the cows in the lake. What he can "see" is that to be an actor in the world as "seen" from Mount Hatelma, he needs to be a "human being," not a servant. But Matti doesn't participate with Puntila in the rapturous choruses with the maids. Puntila asks, "Doesn't your heart swell at the sight of it all?" Matti clings to irony, "My heart swells at the sight of your forests, Mr. Puntila." He "sees" not the milky-white sands but something owned by his master.

Matti finally refuses to see the world differently. He can only tinker with the dynamic of the relationship of master and servant. He cannot imagine how to change it. It is the conflicted master whom his imagination frees of his boundaries. But Puntila will again be sober. What then will become of his boundaries? This dilemma is real, but we also know he will become drunk again.

Imagination as a tool of emotional form first has to wreck and reconfigure the elements that represent ordinary life and then create a vision that is open to an emotional landscape. Puntila rejoices.

> We're climbing, Matti; Excelsior! Leaving behind us buildings and structures put up by human hands we enter the pure realm of nature, which adopts a more austere countenance. Shake off all your petty cares and abandon yourself to the mighty sensation, Matti! (89)

Imagination puts the world in play, freed momentarily from the burden of the real and the necessary. In the arena of the imagination, the force of emotion creates "as if" experiences that affect our relation to what is "real." Matti holds to the safety of his belief. What is real is his place in the division of humankind into master or servant.

Matti departs from Puntila's estate. He has lost the battle with change started by Eva's proposal. Brecht deepens the critique of the master-servant relationship by showing the emotional consequences of the failure of imagination, the failure of its need for a fierce independence and rejection of the slavish gesture. By creating his subject matter from the problems of the social order, Brecht also shows that the world is profoundly important. The emotional form of the play is framed within the choices forced on the character. Epic theater aims to keep our focus on how the social world informs all choice. The rough objectivity that epic theater crafts maintains this focus by creating devices of distance between the audience and the emotion in the narrative, such as, scene shifts, songs, third-person address, and storytelling. Without emotional meaning undergirding the narrative, such distancing lessens dramatic presence and flattens the dramatic landscape.

Brecht's art represents a determination to see the world for what it is and to defend humanity's freedom to make it different, to change what seems fixed by the gods, to view misery as made by human hands and not by unknowable forces. He is determined to reveal the gestures of our cooperation with the forces that oppress us, how we bow and welcome the truncheon and the fist, the paymaster and those who tell us what God wants. There is enough in human nature to know and fear without looking to the heavens.

Practice: Testing the Imagination—What If?

The writer uses imagination to work through the dilemmas of emotional form. The tasks of imagination are:

- fearlessly to make mischief and havoc with the elements of ordinary life
- to put into that landscape characters who hold our concern, who carry an emotional charge
- to create out of this configuration a window into the world of the characters
- to bring pleasure as a spinner of tales

Imagination is what the writer has that can transform the burden of the real and the necessary through the stratagem of "what if." What-if carries the writer inside the real, discovering how the details of experience fit together so a character, like Puntila on his mountain, can see into the heart of his desire.

The writer is like a blind person who touches the objects and people of the world of every day and feels a way to the hidden places therein. Like Shakespeare in *King Lear*, the writer uses "Gloucester's sight" to see everything feelingly and uses Poor Tom's ready play to penetrate what is hidden, to challenge despair, inertia, and the madness of events that spiral toward death. What-if can provide a way to create new realities, to jolt the situation past barriers to the end. What-if can mean what if this, or this, or that happened. What if everything we thought was real was not: a character wakes from a dream, or is discovered to be in a hospital reenacting the events in his life, or is actually dead. What-if can mean what if his dead mother or himself as a child enters this world, or what if the character stops speaking, or holds another character hostage.

> What-if can mean what if instead of kissing his girlfriend, he whispers something upsetting, or he cruelly insults her, or instead of just going along with polite conversation the character blurts out paranoid fears, or a secret, or deliberately attacks someone close. What-if can mean what if a character's memories are mangled and he remembers not his own life but someone else's, or a character has done something unthinkable or thinks he has, or a character's beliefs suddenly change, or he decides sleep is not needed, death is not real, reincarnation is a fact. Playing what-if is a sorting and sifting process that is held in check by the writer's intuition. The writer, like the blind person, is feeling for an opening in the material that has just been rearranged by imagination.
>
> Practice this. Use what-if as a can opener to the material of a developing script or as a launching point. Take any part of a play, and find that place where even your writer's mind wanders, and tear that place open to play what-if. Some writers like to pin a play up on a wall so they can be in constant dialogue with the whole, marking places of trouble and divergence for the work of what-if.

Bearings: A Fire That Can Be Touched

The audience is fundamental to the writer. The link between the writer's life and the created characters and events is as real as the link between the audience member's life and the perceived characters and events. Drama is not something turned on and off like a faucet. It has necessary and sufficient conditions to make the imagined life of the play enter into the dynamic play of the audience's inner life. These conditions can be fiercely difficult to construct, as seen in the examples by Edward Albee and Kane. The fire burning in the character's acts can seem untouchable or unreachable to the observer. The discipline of emotional form can itself be harsh on the writer who suffers to go to our blackest desires and needs. But the writer determinedly finds the sequence of acts that reach beyond judgment and condemnation. There is no opportunity for emotional form without going beyond judgment to a joined sympathy with the audience for the flawed wreck that we call humanity.

Knowing another's emotional life is not accomplished in a simple act of naturalistic representation. What we mostly show to others is a mask of our persona, a fixed presentation of the deep conflicts in our character. That mask stays fixed until some desire or threat knocks it loose, revealing not the mask we are familiar with but what lies beneath and fears to be seen. Emotional form is the psychology of the mask. Knocking the mask loose is our secret pleasure. Who else gets to untie their imaginations to find the events and the forces that will dislodge the mask of a loosely or fiercely held persona and show the consequences. The other feature of the discipline of emotional form is its focus on credibility. When Puntila pulls Matti up Mount Hatelma, we are not treated to a gratuitous flight of fancy, a poetic flowering of Puntila's drunken half. We are engaged in the craft of revealing the inside of Matti's character, the pulling away of his mask.

The resistance to what Dionysus represents, our compromise with conflict, the shape implied by endings, and the conditions that connect play to audience are all part of the content, craft, and discipline of emotional form. What do we know now about emotional form? What is fire walking?

5. *The Practice of Fire Walking*

> The Great Question before us is: Are we doomed?
> The Great Question before us is: Will the Past release us?
> The Great Question before us is: Can we Change? In Time?
> And we all desire that Change will come.
> —Tony Kushner, *Angels in America, Part Two: Perestroika*

We've sought the signs of emotional form through the processes of writing and viewing drama. Emotional form is something well known to writers, a key element of their lives, and how they make and respond to stories. We all register the constant ticking of emotional expression, adjusting to the complex web of needs, anxieties, pain, and pleasure that makes us what we are. Socrates says the unexamined life is not worth living. So we pursue self-knowledge, hoping it will explain everything else. *We* are the subjects of which plays are made: the most interesting, difficult, obtuse, and infuriating characters we know, characters whose turbulent but blurred psychological landscapes are canvases marked by the fire lines of emotional form.

We want to know why do we do what we do. We are drawn to the question because we all have pain or grief that trails us like smoke. We act destructively. We search blindly. We panic, not knowing why. We yearn and don't know the object of our yearning. We sacrifice, attack, or flee in the competition of daily life. The landscape of self is the one subject that embraces all others. Our emotions form the fuel of our pursuits, obsessive or otherwise.

The dramatic enterprise demands that we engage the question, "Why?" We know something mysterious is happening—just from being human, from being players in the big and small parts of the narrative of existence. We realize that our knowledge and our feelings are separated, split apart. We know and feel things, but we don't always know why we feel them. We create havoc when, dumb to who we are, we act on feelings separated from the knowledge of what they mean. Great dramas always tell us this, in characters such as Oedipus, Ibsen's Nora, Willy Loman, King Lear. Drama attempts to confront a character divided by some conflict that determines the story's forward motion, promise an ending that reveals some insight into this separation of feeling and knowledge, and show some consequence because the separation is breeched, or not. These are the operational clauses in the contract of emotional form.

Writers' ideas of character are complicated by many factors, such as parents' efforts to see that their children don't become delinquents, by civic and religious forces that erect a wall between acceptable and unacceptable behavior, and by the instinctive impulse to tunnel beneath this wall and to release our demons in our time and in our way. The conflicts that animate us are unique emotional signatures, but writers know this isn't the whole story. Writers piece the story together by stumbling over and often obfuscating the truth of it. The audience wants to see both the visible and the hidden sources of a character's conflicted emotional expression. To see and feel that conflicted truth is to be in the embrace of emotional form

Adrift between Feeling and Knowing

When the separation of feeling and knowledge occurs, the past forces its way through the cracks of this fracture into the present of the character. The behavior that emerges is attached to the barrier between feeling and knowing. Here is an example. The story occurs in a psychologist's office. Carl is married with grown children. He feels estranged and disengaged from his profession as a pathologist.

For some reason, he feels compelled to dress up in women's clothes, which he has done since he was fourteen. His wife knows about it, and so do his children. He feels no sense of sexual deviance; he simply enjoys dressing up as a woman. He has never understood his compulsion. His behavior has made him private and distant. He visits a psychologist at his wife's insistence. His children say they will not bring their grandchildren to visit or allow them to be alone with their grandfather until he deals with his compulsion.

Time passes, and Carl comes dutifully for his visits to the psychologist. Nothing significant emerges. After watching and listening, the psychologist identifies a profound sadness in Carl. He asks him if this is so. The man bursts into tears. It is the first time someone has seen this in him. His family assumed this to be a quirk but part of his everyday persona. Freed by this recognition, Carl is seized with a memory of his sister.

When they were children, they lived across a road from a pecan orchard. Although they were told not to cross the road and not to take pecans from the orchard, they did so anyway. One day, after picking pecans, they started back home. At the edge of the road, they saw a truck coming. Carl started running. When he reached the other side, he turned to see his sister standing frozen in the middle of the road. The truck struck and killed her.

The family's response to the little girl's death was complete denial. They quickly moved to another town. They never mentioned his sister's name again, and no one was allowed to mention her death. There was no grieving process, no ritual, nothing. The event was erased. Through telling this story to his psychologist, Carl realizes that when he puts on women's clothes, it is as if she is still alive. The only time he feels peace is when he is dressed as a woman. The performance of dressing in women's clothes frees him from his sadness and guilt and undoes the death of his sister. It creates a mute kind of theater that can go no further because there is no one to share it with; the audience has left believing the play is over. Carl's family's denial of his sister's death fractured the connection between knowing and feeling and created his compulsion to dress as a woman. Carl's performance continually enacted the feeling she was still alive. For Carl, the moment of character change came when someone recognized his sadness. Acknowledging this emotion released the story of loss. Voicing the story and breaking the silence imposed by the past brought knowledge and feeling together again.

Emotional form creates a visible smoke rising from the heat in a character's animating conflict. People ordinarily try to leave this smoke in place, with the flame hidden. Drama tries to find a way to reveal the flame to renew life's journey or burn the place to the ground. Drama makes a poetic world. It is not constrained by decorum, representation, or time. Drama looks at character as if we all carry within us a conflict that may either kill or redeem us.

Vital Signs

Drama begins with a glitch in everyday life: where the unexpected threatens the commonplace. A crisis is introduced, bringing the uneasy realization that what was hitherto safe will soon be safe no longer. A character may confront a truth about himself or about someone, someone whose character has always been beyond question—but suddenly is not.

The co-conspirators of emotional form are the writer, the performer, and the audience, who meet on a common human landscape. Assuming resistance is removed, this encounter allows a drama to have its way with an audience. Catharsis is an essential part of this meeting. The way the writer structures the events of plot separates a character's destructive actions from revulsion and condemnation and creates a basis for empathy and for the audience to experience the full range of human folly and catastrophe. To accomplish this, the play must be more than a progression of shocks, excitements to the system, or close encounters with disaster.

The term *plot* is the nervous system of emotional form. Emotional form is the writer's real and fictional emotional lives embedded in the narrative cells of plot to shape its progress. At the same time, plot is the arrangement of narrative events. Emotional form is the psychological and imaginative thinking that create the orderly devices of plot, the march of choices and events that grow into life and become a character's story. What is the break between knowing and feeling, and at what price for the character? What is the threat that jars open an intransigent conflict? What is the arc of change that threads through the events? These are the questions that emotional form must exhaustively work through to understand the purpose for each narrative event and to create an emotionally integrated plot.

Searching the Face of Catastrophe

When we talk about a story that is told in a theater, it is useful to remember it is a practice of storytelling that is not as old as gesture and movement. As Westerners, our habits of dramatic storytelling go back to Greece in the sixth century. That is tens of thousands of years after the animal images carved on the walls of caves and eons later than the dancers and singers seeking the ecstatic or the fertility of nature. Stories that are constructed specifically for what we call theater began with the Greeks. Before Stanley loved Stella, before Nora shut the door, before Mother Courage showed up with her wagon, before Hamlet put on his antic disposition, Clytemnestra murdered Agamemnon in his bath, and Oedipus blinded himself when he discovered the murderer of Laius. We can build upon Aeschylus's understanding of drama with the Renaissance passion of Hamlet holding a mirror to nature. Hamlet talks about how the actor should tell the story but not about how the dramatist makes that story. For Hamlet, the story is something like a foundation he can adapt to his purpose by some casual editing. Hamlet listens to a speech he's asked the player to recite, but it is not the part he was looking for, "Say on: come to Hecuba." And so he does, telling of the disheveled and frenzied Hecuba, a pitiable witness to her husband's death.

> Is it not monstrous that this player here,
> But in a fiction, in a dream of passion,
> Could force his soul so to his own conceit
> That from her working all his visage wanned,

Tears in his eyes, distraction in his aspect,
A broken voice, and his whole function suiting
With forms to his conceit? And all for nothing!
For Hecuba!
What's Hecuba to him, or he to Hecuba
That he should weep for her? (3.2.522)

Stung by the player's display of emotion, Hamlet is goaded to face the true reason for his high feeling. The play's and the player's power over feeling catch Hamlet where reason could not and sets him in motion toward discovery and the end.

The beginnings of drama are drunk with the power of this force. We often don't want to go there, those Greeks killing their children, slitting mother's throat, and gouging out eyes. Drama in its beginnings is eruptive, shattering the surface of things in the amnesiac present. Are blood and sex and betrayal at the root of family life? My family has had its faults, but they haven't gone that far, have they?

Hard Heads, Wrecked Hearts

Without the sustaining power of our emotional response to drama, even more theaters will be turned into strip malls, casinos, and storefront churches. Great plays of the Western repertory all confront their central characters with the unthinkable, breaking them open to events that would not have occurred without the force of their secrets, obsessions, and fears. They find themselves at the edge of the abyss, but what is it that draws us, safe and comfortable in our seats, to gaze into it with them? Why is this connection between the play and the pits of our stomachs our most vital experiences: what's Hecuba to us? Because it is the human emotion that matters most, not plot, not ideas, language, or beauty, though all of them contribute. It is the shape of feeling in the dramatic architecture that holds our gaze, turning it inward.

A writer can borrow emotion from the narratives of other people's lives, but one of the most important steps for a writer is the unqualified confronting and acceptance of self, transforming the work into something personal and distinctive. The writer is easily distracted from seeking either his own or his play's emotional life. The reason a writer writes a play may be merely to create an ironic, engaging conversation for literate people. Emotion that leaves teeth marks is seldom the invited guest to the smart dinner party; it can break the dishes and overturn the careful order and occasion of the table. Everything conspires to make the writer steer clear of her most troublesome emotions when she starts to write. Writers are advised that feeling will happen by itself; it will arise from the characters if the writer only makes them real enough. Or it comes from beneath the surface of the characters' interactions and will arise or happen if the writer has a workable plot. The truth is, creating emotional presence is personally difficult. It arouses resistance and the fear of being exposed or violated. It is the hard, hard work audiences want writers to do.

The dramatist's greatest asset is the willingness to go deeply into his own private world, there to explore the dimly lit corners of his own struggle and to confront those painful situations where the only options were surrender or denial. The committed writer must revisit the deepest feelings, the most intractable resentments, the most passionate and impractical ideals, and transmute them into characters who will breathe life into them. The "hidden hand" of emotional form is not hidden at all. It is the writer's own hand, guided by the writer's core emotions into the determining causality of dramatic architecture. The seed of the character's emotional journey lives somewhere inside the writer, waiting for the call to action so it may emerge in a series of events and choices that are the visible shape of the writer's struggle with the dynamics of his own life's emotional form.

Practice: Keep It in the Room

No one can take the writer to the place of emotional life except the writer. When the writer feels the heat in that room, there is a strong impulse to pull away and let it slip out the door. Keep it in the room. When encountering the knot of a character's conflicted feeling, the impulse is often to deflect it, to change the subject as in a jump cut or to create distance as in epic theater. The room in this case is the character's conflicts past, present, and future. Going off on brilliant monologues, or traveling to alternate realities, or engaging in theatrical hi-jinks that fail to engage the conflict is leaving the room. The test is, can you feel the link between what you've written and the character's troubling conflict? Feel it, do not explain the link, no matter how easy. Perhaps you don't know what the trouble is or what the room is or whether you're inside or outside. Give definition to the room. Sometimes, the obvious is the most useful place to go, like checking whether the computer is plugged in. What is the script about? It is a question you either asked or raced past at the beginning. Answering this is not necessarily useful. Also not useful are the script reader's one-liners: "Kooky family finds happiness after night of matchmaking and trouble," or "Secret of marriage bed blinds son in terrible discovery." If the writer doesn't answer the "about" question, he cannot know whether he has stayed in the room or fled to the garden to swoon among the hydrangeas. Just try to answer the question until you stop writing: Why did you stop? Another way to answer the "about" question is to make a metaphoric picture of this room. Create a collage on a poster-board-sized paper on the wall. Create a line across the paper that represents the base time line from beginning to end. Using pictures, some words, found material, and references to sound, construct a picture of the emotional journey of the character's trouble. The purpose of the collage, like readings and feedback, is to help the writer discover the places of avoidance—and mystery—to find a way through them to use the resistance.

The Furies' Path

Artists use the word *form* to emphasize that what they do is a shaping and is essentially creative. In drama, form contains the events that create the emotional meaning of a character's response to the plot but only when the gap is closed between a character's feeling and knowing. Emotional form is fully revealed when the narrative is complete, and the end is in place. What do we mean when we say, "Hamlet"? Do we mean the whole play in all its theatrical specificity, or do we mean a particular emotional expression of the prince's fierce conflict, conflict made up of duty, self-loathing, and doubt that cause a series of events to unfold? We see in this unfolding the emotional form of Shakespeare's *Hamlet.*

Form as used by artists is not an empty abstraction. Susanne K. Langer in her book *Feeling and Form* presents the difference between empty and full.

> Yet forms are either empty abstractions, or they do have a content; and artistic forms have a very special one, namely their import. They are logically expressive, or significant, forms. They are symbols for the articulation of feeling, and convey the elusive and yet familiar pattern of sentience. . . . They belong to the same category as language, though their logical form is a different one, and as myth and dream, though their function is not the same. (52)

Creating the sequence of events in a play is not "One damn thing after another," but "One damn thing *because* of another." Understanding a character is only possible after we've seen him blown about across a full spectrum of the winds of event and opposition. The writer makes progress insofar as the central character's story is contained by a shaping form, a language made from desire, loss, and fear that is sometimes like myth and dream. It is a language that determines our connection to others. The writer builds this language from behavior in a dynamic process. The writer's work on plot and emotional form emerges; it is not prefigured or planned as in a recipe. No numbered instructions come with this package, and "secrets here revealed" writing seminar can substitute for this work.

In her heart, the writer knows that configured in her own conflicted vitality is a way of seeing character and behavior. The writer's life is marked by conflict whose causes and matter determine how past and present intersect in the world. It is the mystery of her own character, comprising will, desire, and loss that fuel the need to write.

The dramatist has one thing in common with the priest: he or she must learn to love and accept all creatures that aspire to being called human. That dictator, that murderer, that monster can't be worthy subjects of a play. But they are. Narrative shaped by emotional form thrives in the empathic recognition that something the writer can imagine as part of human experience is played out before an audience in unexpected and revealing ways. It is to the priest one confesses the dark deeds of one's secret life and awaits the penance. The dramatist disavows judgment and sees how these same acts animate a dramatic character. This character's acts are revealed in a pattern of events that become part of the audience's shared experience and inner life and thus are freed to emerge in a multitude of meanings.

Story Junkies

Human action takes many forms, driven by desire for some knowledge, some bargain with survival, some belief. Narrative is the way we try to penetrate the meaning of such actions, separate them from the chaos of existence and of our own consciousness, and organize them into a sequence that we can understand.

We don't come to a story empty-handed. We bring an expectation of how it might end, an expectation both prurient and pristine. Our sense of life is greatest when everything is put at risk by a conflict that threatens the imminent wreck of good intentions. This sense of disaster is at once everywhere and highly refined. It lives among an abundance of tale-telling strategies that want our attention. As listeners, our own needs are large and complicated and not always clear or admirable. We will listen to gossip and wait for the hit of pleasure, that we are somehow a different species than the craven, the unlucky, the foolish, the willful. We listen for the voice of the herd to catechize this difference, the burning of an effigy that we can unite against.

A story also can be a kind of animated cartoon of the imagination. Characters intentionally cruel or evil are allowed to run amok until a noble stereotype, standing in for justice, strikes them down. The stuff of pubescent fantasy morphs into morality tales and primetime police theater. Such tales are unquestionably satisfying. We can express our anger or our approval of unproblematic figures, rub them like a psychic talisman to get a fix. It is the video version of Chinese food. Half an hour later, you're hungry for another episode of *CSI*.

The Drumbeat of Time

Langer relates time to plot.

> It has been said repeatedly that the theater creates a perpetual present moment; but it is only a present filled with its own future that is really dramatic. A sheer immediacy, an imperishable direct experience without the ominous forward movement of consequential action, would not be so. As literature creates a virtual past, drama creates a virtual future. The literary mode is the mode of Memory; the dramatic is the mode of Destiny. (307)

Destiny may be the forward-leaning cant of the story, but change is the engine that drives it. Change is when character breaks loose from his emotional moorings. It either destroys him utterly, leaving the stage stacked with corpses, or creates knowledge that nothing ever will be the same.

The making of plot also can be like a dead hand, cheating us of the rich confusions and mysteries of life. Peter Brooks in *Reading for the Plot* echoes this.

> If we cannot do without plots, we nonetheless feel uneasy about them, and feel obliged to show up their arbitrariness, to parody their mechanisms while admitting our dependence on them. Until such a time as we cease to exchange understandings in the form of stories, we will need to remain dependent on the logic we use to shape and to understand stories, which is to say, dependent on plot. A reflection on plot as the syntax of a certain way of speaking our understanding of the world may tell us something about how and why we have come to stake so many of the central concerns of our society, and of our lives, on narrative. (7)

Emotional form masters the functions of plot by harnessing those functions to determine content and meaning. Narrative is the flow of events unmarked by the troubles of the plot. Brecht's Galy Gay goes out one day to buy a fish and by night has taken on the identity of a missing soldier, Jeriah Jip. Narrative event occurs in time and is like the bolt of cloth from which a particular dramatic suit is cut. Plot provides the cut and design of that suit. Narrative provides the weave, color, and the feel of the material. Plot is the writer's cut of the events of the narrative.

Emotional form is rooted in a conception of the individual that regards our present life as a confluence of instincts that create the volatile flux that is our complex, conflicted emotional life. The writer works to make known a turbulence behind the mask of narrative, a turbulence that also belongs to the writer. Like the writer, character is divided between a resistant, threatening inner world and a separate, dangerous outer world. The work of plot is to grasp this division and hammer it into a meaning and resolution. This resolution may be inadequate, horrific, or satisfying.

Change Is All

Emotional form is inextricably tied to the events of change in a play. It is necessarily hidden from the central character because it is unknown. At the outset, characters are animated by will, driving them toward what they desire. Change demands that a truth come out, not in the safety of a fantasy, but when least expected or wanted. Two threads of emotional form divide into two distinct forces: the character's desire and the specific nature of his ignorance. The character's ignorance includes whom he fears, loves, and hates, along with his feelings about himself, which he may accommodate or may deny to make them bearable. The pressure of the divisions in the character propels the narrative forward but only to the middle. To create an end, the pressure must coalesce in some experience that reshapes the character's ignorance, transforming the meaning of this division in the character. As in life, it doesn't remove the division. Change that removes this division is the stuff of cartoons and fantasy.

The tension between surface activity and the forces building beneath it marks the interplay between above and below the neck, the rational and irrational spheres of the character. Because we know this separation exists between our own inner and outer selves, our trust of what people tell us depends on the test of action. When we see a character threatened, when something is desired and demanded—obedience, affection, love, allegiance, silence, betrayal—we want to see what happens. Language is a tool used as often to deceive others as to reveal. A character's speech becomes dramatically interesting because we recognize it as part of a mask. The main purpose of the mask is to keep the character's deep conflict at a calculated emotional distance, a distance built from compromises with the past. Emotional form is the only way to express the deepest levels of a character's conflict. Emotional form seeks the relentless trouble that disrupts the linkage of desire and conflict and thus unleashes change. Dramatic change is a test of the vitality and consequence in a play's theme, its structure, and its ending all wished for and feared by the audience, who act as collaborators of meaning.

The Insistence of Change: *Angels in America*

Tony Kushner's play *Angels in America* is an example of the power unleashed in dramatic narratives of change that can alter our sense of self, purpose, and place. The play exemplifies: (a) the deep structure of emotional form and its use of psychological language to find meaning, (b) the social structure of emotional form as encounter with the world, and (c) the use of imagination in expanding the psychological into languages of dream and myth.

Confronting the experience of change, that is, its assault on our knowledge of ourselves, creates wildly differing outcomes. It brings to mind the circle of dancers in a long-ago Greek meadow in a pandemonium of sound that ceases suddenly as the dancers sway in silence, waiting for the ecstatic moment in which the transformative god Dionysus enters their beings. Ecstatic dance ritual is one way we have accommodated the forces that war in our bodies. Theater and drama are others. Drama cheats time by taking the force of change that is overwhelming in its impact, chaotic and unbidden as it takes its toll and slows it all down, replays and sequences what was scattered into narrative, what was silence into thought, what was private into shared feeling.

In *Angels in America*, we enter a vast and ancient struggle for love and justice, for purchase and meaning of place in the American civic space, for God in a landscape of plague, destruction, and denial. The movement of change in the play cascades through the characters: Prior sick with AIDS and abandoned by Louis; Harper lost to herself and to her marriage to Joe; Joe divided by what he wants and what he serves; Roy, Rabelaisian in his appetites for wielding and keeping power, Jesuitical in naming what he is, and ferocious in claiming his pleasures; Louis frightened out of love by the mess of sickness and in love with the distancing and moralizing of big ideas; Hanna, who wants to endure all suffering to hold it in check before it can corrode belief and meaning; Belize, who knows the difference between sick and well and how to fight for spreading the wealth; and finally the Angel and her legions frantic with God's abandonment and spiraling backwards as a hapless counterweight to humanity's headlong, blind motion. Change happens, change rips through the fabric of this narrative, uprooting characters from their place of identity and order, from their own bodies and values, from the people they thought they loved, from life itself. At the center of this churning dynamic is America as idea, spiritual record, and dream landscape of preachers, pioneers, fools, fags, thugs, lawyers, and housewives.

The Anglo-Saxon God, whether of the white clapboard, steepled churches, or of the visionaries of the desert and the mountains, or the binding force symbolized on currency of the nation's good, has fled. His angel, who is powerful, sensual, full of the trappings of ancient language and disturbance of air and matter, has come only to tell those confronted with the plague to stop moving, that stasis is required to bring God back. It is a message of the unhuman, a dead letter no one can accept. One part of the America in this two-part play is claimed and narrated by Roy Cohn as the figure freest to claim his sway, his right, his need. He is a master contender for the prize of grasping the balls of power and sticking his tongue down the throat of truth. Words countered by deeds preserve his kind of freedom. For Roy, truth is good for fucking other people. Prior acknowledges the Roy effect: "mostly the truth fucks you." Roy's aggression, paternalism, charm, cunning, and danger make a restless, timeless claim to a swaggering, confident I-got-mine-screw-you America.

Not so clear is the other part of this America, the anti-Roy America. This other part emerges from the crossing stories of Harper and Joe, Hanna, Louis and Prior, Joe and Prior, and the Angel, set in motion by the appearance of lesions on Prior's body. This initiates the play: a rupture in the body's integrity, its future, its past, and its self-knowledge. Rabbi Chemelwitz speaks of the immigrants' bodies carrying a reality that never melted into this American place. He describes the body as a geography of things gained and lost.

> You do not live in America. No such place exists. Your clay is the clay of some Litvak shtetl, your air the air of the steppes—because she carried the old world on her back across the ocean, in a boat, and she put it down on Grand Concourse Avenue, or in Flatbush, and she worked that earth into your bones, and you pass it to your children, this ancient, ancient culture and home. (*Part One*, 10)

The body, smudged by the dirt of time, feared and damned from the pulpit, laid waste by greed, by visions, by need, and celebrated by His heavenly angels is the site of this play's struggle with change.

ROY: I wish I was an octopus, a fucking octopus. Eight loving arms and all those suckers. Know what I mean? (*Part One*, 11)

HARPER: People are like planets, you need a thick skin. Things get to me, Joe stays away and no. . . . Well look. My dreams are talking back to me. (*Part One*, 17–18)

PRIOR: I can't find a way to spare you, baby. No wall like the wall of hard scientific fact. K. S. Wham. Bang your head on that. (*Part One*, 22)

LOUIS (*Answering the question why would a person abandon someone he loves in a time of great need.*): Maybe because this person's sense of the world, that I will change for the better with the struggle, maybe a person who has this neo-Hegelian positivist sense of constant historical progress towards happiness or perfection or something, who feels very powerful because he feels connected to these forces, moving uphill all the time . . . maybe that person can't, um, incorporate sickness into his sense of how things are supposed to go. Maybe vomit . . . and sores and disease . . . really frighten him, maybe . . . he isn't so good with death. (*Part One*, 25)

ANGEL: You are mere Flesh. I I I I am Utter Flesh, Density of Desire, the Gravity of Skin: What makes the Engine of Creation Run? Not Physics But Ecstatics Makes The Engine Run: . . . The Body is the Garden of the Soul. (*Part Two*, 47)

The body betrays us. Love betrays us. Who is betraying the country? God betrays us, and we betray God. Harper says, "But everywhere, things are collapsing, lies surfacing, systems of defense giving way. . . . This is why Joe, this is why I shouldn't be left alone." Nor do we want to be left alone. We may not believe all things are collapsing, but we fear it. We may not have our own Mr. Lies, but we know we could. Lodged in us are the events of our lives that grind and churn in our guts until we voice the feelings they carry. These feelings are not ideas. They are mysterious and energizing when they escape the control of the explainer, the ironist, the apologist, and the fixer. These are feelings strong enough to allow us to chew down a tree with our teeth.

With a simple action of a man going to buy a fish, Brecht shows how this same man with a bit of pressure can be convinced to swap his identity for that of a bloody-minded machine fighting for Queen and Empire. A man's a man, good for this one minute, but what about the next? Kushner's Prior Walter gets up one morning and is marked. Unlike Galy Gay, he is already marked as a gay man in Ronald Reagan's America. Kushner calls his story "A Gay Fantasia on National Themes." Kushner's achievement is in creating the emotional force of this fantasia that takes apart the pieties of our American life, our furious pilgrim's progress, and exposes its cruel, frightened center. The play moves us in its ambition, the sweep of its concerns, the reality of its characters' struggles and pain, the sharp tonic of its wit and humor, the language and imagination of the spiritual crisis that is Prior's journey, the embrace of the civic and political world that defines us as a body politic, sick or well. It is as if Arthur Miller and Bertolt Brecht became fused in Kushner's mind and then were joined to the cosmological and lyrical by a Ben Jonson who was Walt Whitman's lover.

Angels in America is many things to those who experience it. It is the great American play exposing the spiritual fevers in the American body politic, a body that is fought over by gays and straights in the name of love. It is history's body, burned by visions of angels and visions of promise, plenty, and the righteous life. It is a play of Shakespearian scope in an American voice: skeptical, irreverent, deeply spiritual, creating characters marked by their time, the furies of power, of love, and of right as acted out in the context of the AIDS disaster, a rent in the fabric of life that yields cosmic dreams. But what is the core of this narrative?

Mangled Guts Pretending

The core of Kushner's epic and the core of its emotional form are the question that Harper asks the Mormon mother. It is the question every playwright needs to ask: "In your experience of the world. How do people change?"

MORMON MOTHER: Well it has something to do with God so it's not very nice. God splits the skin with a jagged thumbnail from throat to belly and then plunges a huge filthy hand in, he grabs hold of your bloody tubes and they slip to evade his grasp but he squeezes hard, he *insists*, he pulls and pulls till all your innards are yanked out and the pain! We can't even talk about that. And then he stuffs them back, dirty, tangled and torn. It's up to you to do the stitching.

HARPER: And then get up. And walk around.

MORMON MOTHER: Just mangled guts pretending.
HARPER: That's how people change. (*Part Two*, 79)

Drama can take many forms, the imagination being what it is, but it cannot evade the question, How do people change? As seen in the Mormon Mother's answer, change is an agent of emotional upheaval and physical pain, pressed by such force as to be undeniable. Kushner's "mangled guts pretending" is a description that could be applied to the ends of most dramas.

The Greeks had their own version of God's thumbnail. You are driving down the road with the top down. The heat haze blurs the seam between sky and earth. You come over the crest of a small hill, and there is a man walking stiffly along the side of the road. You stop and offer the traveler a ride. Just because he was there, you take him in. After all, you're going in the same direction.

"So your name is Oedipus. Seems like I've heard of you." You slow for a crossroads looming ahead.

"Stop!" he orders. "I'll walk from here." He walks toward the crossroads, and you realize a vehicle is approaching from the opposite direction. It slows and stops, blocking the intersection.

What do you do? Shout, "Stop, Oedipus, you're going to make a terrible mistake." Or do you drive a little closer to get a better view?

Of course, you're going to move closer to the action to see what happens. At that moment, you toss out the window the old road map marked "Fate." It is not fate you want to see, it is Oedipus, willfully intact.

Or think of a racetrack. In one car is Oedipus, and in another car are the prophecy and the events of the drama's fulfillment, Apollo at the throttle. The hero lives his life on this speedway. His speed, power, and courage set him apart from the rest of us. We know all about how well heroes and heroines have raced in the past. The audience comes to admire the prowess of the driver, but they equally watch so they can see the champion hit the guardrail and burst into flames. Oedipus presses toward the discovery of the murderer of Laius, saying, "My own good . . . I'll have none of it."

Then on cue, Apollo, driving his own disaster machine in the opposite direction, roars into view and swerves head-on into the hero's path.

> O, O,
> where am I going? Where is my voice
> borne on the wind to and fro?
> Spirit, how far have you sprung? (*Oedipus*, 68)

The chorus echoes the shudder of emotion we feel. Human life is vulnerable to unpredictable change that is capable of sweeping away reason, accomplishment, and happiness. But it is change unfiltered by easy categories of judgment. Each of us must grapple with what change means to us, just as our bloodied and wrecked hero must struggle with it as he emerges from the burning hulk of a previous life. This is a powerful freedom, to determine in this crucible of suffering the meaning that will be applied to one's life. This is the genius of putting the cause of disaster in a separate car, so that the hero and the people who suffer the blows will practice the courage to make new meaning and not be satisfied with prescriptions from the past.

Change is the question with which the writer wrestles from the beginning. Change is the reality we all seek to deny. Desire for change is what is embedded in conflict, and the fear of change is what divides feeling from knowledge in character—the state of blindness known since Oedipus. Change of the deepest import is always internal; it is formed by what puts our humanity at risk. Change rips people apart and rips apart societies and civilizations as well. Change is a condition, not a choice. The writer charts it, tries to see the truth of it. Understanding your task as a writer takes you to the place where you can feel God's hand on your innards.

But what can I do? As the Mormon Mother says, "You ain't stupid. So don't ask stupid. Ask for something real." Ask yourself to know something real about yourself and your characters. You are what you read, what you feel, what you know, what you experience. You never stop working on this. This is art, not inventory. Harper and Prior see the Mormon diorama come to life with Joe and Louis mixed into it.

HARPER: (*Pointing to Mormon Mother.*) His wife. His mute wife. I'm waiting for her to speak. Bet her story's not so jolly.

PRIOR: Imagination is a dangerous thing.

HARPER: (*Looking at the father dummy.*) In certain circumstances, fatal. It can blow up in your face. If it turns out to be true. Threshold . . .

PRIOR AND HARPER: . . . of revelation. (*Part Two*, 70)

Aristotle, realism, naturalism, expressionism, surrealism, epic theater, modernism, postmodernism, and all the rest: the imagination feeds on these, as on leftovers from a big party to which you weren't invited. But there is a party you are invited to: working, loving, grieving, yearning, making, fearing, praying, despairing, connecting. . . . If you ever wondered about imagination's purpose in drama, Kushner can help you.

Imagination is an instrument of emotional form, extending the poetic world driven by character and the forces of change. Prior Walter's encounter with the angel may be a fever dream, but it is also a rolling sermon on our spiritual existence and the body as the site of struggle of the ecstatic. So what can the writer do? Do the work that exposes your feelings, your weaknesses, your anger, your beliefs, your doubts, and your heart. Too bad if that's what you already know you have to do. Too bad it is so hard. Too bad there are no sure-fire tricks. No one is making you write but yourself.

Final Bearings: Seeing Beyond the Mirror

When we try to understand the process of change in a drama, we are simply looking for the shape of emotional form, how feeling and knowledge split and become conflicted in a character's journey, creating a disruptive need to bring the two together, a need to find out, Why do we do what we do?

Here are two ways to think of the calamity of choosing to write. First, it is the calamity we see and experience by being human: our grand gestures, our blind failings, our fierce needs and cruel acts, our pain and loss, our luminous love, our laughter at our absurdity. Second, it is the calamity of death. This is harder to explain. The dead are our ghosts. But among us are many who teeter dangerously close to becoming the living dead. We grieve for the first and fear to become the second. The theater is a unique place where we can experience the pain and loss of death; then we, and the dead, can put on our coats and go have a drink together.

But there is something else. To make the stories that feign death, we want to pursue and know every shred of what makes us alive. We want to be the never-satisfied practitioners of feigning life. We writers are only any good if we can show how precious and surprising is that life we share and what it costs not to know the difference between alive and dead. We are only good to ourselves if we don't stop, if we keep trying to grasp the calamity of our humanity, if we keep rushing on to the next story. We are besotted with stories; we can't shut up, we won't shut up, and we are afraid. We are afraid that if we stop talking, writing, playing, dancing, we will forget what's alive and free in us, forget to face what we fear to write. All of us who claim to be writers are messengers, and the messages we bring can, I promise you, make a difference. What is a message? Is it a note in a bottle washed up on a shore distant from its starting place? Is it warnings and alarums? Is it *j'accuse*? Or is it the language that carries the truth of actually experienced feeling. We can all shout and rend our clothes, kick over the furniture, and bellow like a bull. It's easy to frighten the children, but can you make them laugh, feel delight, surprise, or wonder? You can't put that in a bottle. It is alive in your telling of the tale. It is in Kushner's instinct to cut out all the blubbering over ourselves, to have enough wit and self-awareness when God's angel crashes into our room to tell it to piss off. It is cumulative; there can never be enough stories, enough efforts to know ourselves, enough writers. Writers, you make of yourselves a literate army, there will always be plenty of the other kind. Like Prior, you can't stop moving. Seek, as he says, "*More life.* The Great Work Begins."

Bibliography
Index

Bibliography

Albee, Edward. *The Goat or Who Is Sylvia?* New York: Overlook, 2000.

Aristotle. *Poetics*. Trans. Gerald F. Else. Ann Arbor: U of Michigan P, 1970.

———. *Poetics*. Trans. Richard Janko. Indianapolis: Hackett, 1987.

Bergson, Henri. *Laughter*. In *Comedy*. Ed. Wylie Sypher. Baltimore: John's Hopkins UP, 1956. 61–190.

Blau, Herbert. *The Audience*. Baltimore: Johns Hopkins UP, 1990.

———. "Hysteria, Crabs, Gospel, and Random Access: Ring around the Audience." *Studies in the Literary Imagination* 21 (Fall 1988): 7–22.

Bold, Alan. *Harold Pinter: You Never Heard Such Silence*. Totowa, NJ: Barnes & Noble, 1984.

Bullough, Edward. "'Psychical Distance' as a Factor in Art and as an Aesthetic Principle." *British Journal of Psychology* 5 (1912): 87–117.

Brecht, Bertolt. *Bertolt Brecht Poems, 1913–1956*. Ed. John Willett and Ralph Mannheim. New York: Routledge, 1979.

———. *Brecht on Theatre*. Trans. John Willett. New York: Hill and Wang, 1964.

———. *Drums in the Night*. In *Bertolt Brecht Collected Plays*. Ed. Ralph Manheim and John Willett. New York: Vintage, 1971. 59–106.

———. *Mr. Puntila and His Man Matti*. Trans. John Willet. Ed. John Willet and Ralph Mannheim. New York: Arcade, 1997.

Brenner, Charles. *The Mind in Conflict*. New York: International Universities P, 1982.

Brooks, Peter. *Psychoanalysis and Storytelling*. Cambridge: Blackwell, 1994.

———. *Reading for the Plot: Design and Intention in Narrative*. Cambridge: Harvard UP, 1984.

Brownstein, Oscar Lee. *Strategies of Drama: The Experience of Form*. Westport, CT: Greenwood, 1991.

Brownstein, Oscar Lee, and Darlene M. Dauber. *Analytical Sourcebook of Concepts in Dramatic Theory*. Westport, CT: Greenwood, 1981.

Burkman, Katherine H. *The Dramatic World of Harold Pinter: Its Basis in Ritual*. Columbus: Ohio State UP, 1971.

Burkman, Katherine H., and John Kundert-Gibbs, eds. *Pinter at Sixty*. Bloomington: Indiana UP, 1993.

Bly, Carol. *The Passionate Accurate Story*. Minneapolis: Milkweed, 1998.

Carroll, Lewis. *Alice's Adventures in Wonderland*. New York: Random, 1965.

Cartwright, Rosalind. *Night Life: Explorations in Dreaming*. Englewood Cliffs: Prentice-Hall, 1977.

Castagno, Paul. *New Playwriting Strategies: A Language Based Approach to Playwriting*. New York: Routledge, 2001.

Chekhov, Anton. *Uncle Vanya*. Trans. Anne Dunnigan. In *Chekhov: The Major Plays*. New York: New Amer. Lib., 1964. 171–231.

Cixous, Hélène. *Three Steps on the Ladder of Writing*. Trans. Sarah Cornell and Susan Sellers. New York: Columbia UP, 1993.

Diamond, Elin. *Pinter's Comic Play*. Cranbury: Bucknell UP, 1985.

Dukore, Bernard F. *Harold Pinter.* London: Macmillan, 1988.
Egri, Lajos. *The Art of Dramatic Writing: Its Basis in the Creative Interpretation of Human Motives.* New York: Simon, 1960.
Else, Gerald. *Aristotle:* Poetics. Ann Arbor: U of Michigan P, 1970.
———. *Aristotle's* Poetics*: The Argument.* Cambridge: Harvard UP, 1957.
———. *The Origin and Early Form of Greek Tragedy.* New York: Norton, 1965.
Euripides. *Bacchae.* Trans. Paul Woodruff. Indianapolis: Hackett, 1998.
———. *The Bacchae.* In *The Complete Greek Tragedies.* Vol. 4. Ed. David Grene and Richard Lattimore. Chicago: U of Chicago P, 1958. 543–608.
Fortier, Mark. *Theory/Theatre: An Introduction.* New York: Routledge, 1997.
Freud, Sigmund. *The Basic Writings of Sigmund Freud.* Trans. and ed. A. A. Brill. New York: Mod. Lib., 1938.
Fuchs, Elinor. *The Death of Character: Perspectives on Theater after Modernism.* Bloomington: Indiana UP, 1996.
Fuegi, John. *Brecht and Company: Sex, Politics, and the Making of the Modern Drama.* New York: Grove, 1994.
Fugard, Athol. *"MASTER HAROLD" . . . and the boys.* New York: Penguin, 1982.
———. *Notebooks 1960–1977.* New York: Theatre Communications Group, 1983.
Ibsen, Henrik. *A Doll's House.* Version by Frank McGuinness. Trans. Charlotte Barslund. London: Faber, 1996.
Gabbard, Lucina Paquet. *The Dream Structure of Pinter's Plays: A Psychoanalytic Approach.* Cranbury: Associated UP, 1976.
Gablik, Suzi. *Has Modernism Failed?* New York: Thames, 1984.
Gale, Stephen H. *Butter's Going Up: A Critical Analysis of Harold Pinter's Work.* Durham: Duke UP, 1977.
———. *Harold Pinter Critical Approaches.* Cranbury: Associated UP, 1986.
Gardner, John. *The Art of Fiction.* New York: Random, 1985.
Hatcher, Jeffrey. *The Art & Craft of Playwriting.* Cincinnati: Story, 1996.
Hayman, Ronald. *Harold Pinter.* New York: Ungar, 1973.
Holland, Norman N. "Unity Identity Text Self." In *Reader-Response Criticism.* Ed. Jane P. Tompkins. Baltimore: Johns Hopkins UP, 1980. 118–33.
Krutch, Joseph Wood. *"Modernism" in Modern Drama.* New York: Russell, 1962.
Kushner, Tony. *Angels in America, Part One: Millennium Approaches.* New York: Theatre Communications Group, 1992.
———. *Angels in America, Part Two: Perestroika.* New York: Theatre Communications Group, 1992.
Lakoff, George, and Mark Johnson. *Philosophy in the Flesh: The Embodied Mind and Its Challenge to Western Thought.* New York: Basic, 1999.
Langer, Susanne K. *Feeling and Form: A Theory of Art.* New York: Scribner's, 1953.
MacLeod, Alistair. *Island: The Complete Stories.* New York: Norton, 2001.
Margulies, Donald. *The Loman Family Picnic.* In *Sight Unseen and Other Plays.* New York: Theatre Communications Group, 1995. 197–264.
Nietzsche, Friedrich. *The Birth of Tragedy and the Genealogy of Morals.* Trans. Francis Golffing. New York: Doubleday, 1956.
O'Neill, Eugene. *Long Day's Journey into Night.* New Haven: Yale UP, 1956.
Paris, Bernard J. *Imagined Human Beings.* New York: New York UP, 1997.

Parks, Suzan-Lori. "Elements of Style." In *The America Play and Other Works.* New York: Theatre Communications Group, 1995. 6–18.

Pinter, Harold. *The Birthday Party.* In *Complete Works.* New York: Grove, 1976. 4 vols. 1:17–97.

Schlueter, June. *Dramatic Closure: Reading the End.* Cranbury: Associated UP, 1995.

Segal, Charles. *Dionysiac Poetics and Euripides' Bacchae.* Princeton: Princeton UP, 1982.

Shakespeare, William. *Hamlet.* New York, Dover, 1992.

———. *King Lear.* In *The London Shakespeare.* Vol. 6. Ed. John Munro. New York: Simon, 1957.

Shepard, Sam. *Seven Plays.* New York: Bantam, 1981.

Shinn, Christopher. *What Didn't Happen.* In *Where Do We Live and Other Plays.* New York: Theatre Communications Group, 2005. 121–90.

Sophocles. *Antigone.* In *The Oedipus Cycle.* Trans. by Dudley Fitts and Robert Fitzgerald. New York: Harcourt, 1977. 156–204.

———. *Oedipus the King.* In *Sophocles I: The Complete Greek Tragedies.* Ed. David Grene and Richard Lattimore. Chicago: U of Chicago P, 1954. 9–76.

Steiner, George. *The Death of Tragedy.* London: Faber, 1961.

Sweet, Jeffery. With Stephen Johnson and Sandra Hastie. *Cover.* In *25 Ten-minute Plays from Actors Theatre of Louisville.* New York: French, 1989. 203–12.

Taylor, John Russell. *The Angry Theatre.* New York: Hill, 1962.

Tzara, Tristan. *Dada Manifesto.* Trans. Barbara Wright. In *Dada Performance.* Ed. Mel Gordon. New York: PAJ, 1987. 45–51.

Wellman, Mac. *Crowtet 1: A Murder of Crows and the Hyacinth Macaw.* Los Angeles: Green, 2000.

Index

Jim Linnell, a professor of theater at the University of New Mexico, is the founder of the MFA in dramatic writing and of the Words Afire Festival, a two-week festival of new plays from the writing program, at UNM. His most recent play, *Plunda*, conceived to take place simultaneously in two theaters linked by video, was produced at UNM.